THE CENTRAL SCHOOL OF SPEECH AND DRAMA
UNIVERSITY OF LONDON

24 OCT 2014

WITHDRAWN

Please return or renew this item by the last date shown.

The Library, Central School of Speech and Drama,
Embassy Theatre, Eton Avenue, London, NW3 3HY
http://heritage.cssd.ac.uk
library@cssd.ac.uk
Direct line: 0207 559 3942

D0259342

Touchstones 2

NEW SCHOOL SERIES

Consulting Editor: R. Stone, M.A., A.Inst.P.,
Second Master, Manchester Grammar School

General Editor (Arts): B. A. Phythian, M.A., B.Litt.,
Headmaster, Langley Park School for Boys, Beckenham

Starting-Points
Creative Writing for Junior Forms
G. P. Fox, M.A.
B. A. Phythian, M.A., B.Litt.

Listen
An Anthology of Dramatic Monologues
W. A. Thompson, M.A.

Storylines
An Anthology of Short Stories
W. A. Thompson, M.A.

Considering Poetry
An Approach to Criticism
Edited by B. A. Phythian, M.A., B.Litt.

Touchstones 2

A TEACHING ANTHOLOGY

M. G. BENTON M.A.
Head of the English Department,
Minchenden School, Southgate

P. BENTON M.A.
Head of the English Department,
The Grammar School, Letchworth

375·821

THE CENTRAL SCHOOL
OF SPEECH TRAINING
AND DRAMATIC ART
LIBRARY.

THE ENGLISH UNIVERSITIES PRESS LTD

Contents

To the Teacher		viii
Creative Writing		x

PART A

SHAPES
Includes:

Breathless	Wilfrid Noyce	3
The Mouse's Tail	Lewis Carroll	6
Calligram (15th May 1915)	G. Apollinaire	7
The Fork	Peter Hunt	8

SOUNDS
Includes:

Jabberwocky	Lewis Carroll	9

RHYTHM AND MOVEMENT
Includes:

The Daniel Jazz	Vachel Lindsay	15
Night Mail	W. H. Auden	18

PART B

SHAPES

The Mosquito	D. H. Lawrence	5
Mountain Lion	D. H. Lawrence	8
In Sunlight	E. E. Cummings	30
One This Snowflake	E. E. Cummings	31
To a Snowflake	Francis Thompson	32
In Just-spring	E. E. Cummings	33
From *The Gecko*	John Heath-Stubbs	34
Johnny Nolan	Lawrence Ferlinghetti	35
The Computer's First Christmas Card	Edwin Morgan	36
On This Island	W. H. Auden	37
Creative Writing		37

SOUNDS

Thunder and Lightning	James Kirkup	40
From *Fall of a Tower*	Francis Berry	41
The Blacksmiths	Anon	43
Elinour Rumming	John Skelton	44
Jazz Fantasia	Carl Sandburg	46
Silences	Thomas Hardy	47
Echo	Walter de la Mare	48
The Splendour Falls	Lord Tennyson	48
Pleasant Sounds	John Clare	50
Creative Writing		51

RHYTHM AND MOVEMENT

Inversnaid	G. M. Hopkins	53
The Quarry	W. H. Auden	53
Tarantella	Hilaire Belloc	55
Skimbleshanks: The Railway Cat	T. S. Eliot	56
Child's Bouncing Song	Tony Connor	58
The Congo	Vachel Lindsay	60
Creative Writing		65

ANIMALS, BIRDS AND INSECTS

Fox	Clifford Dyment	67
Carrion	Clifford Dyment	67
The Jaguar	Ted Hughes	68
The Tyger	William Blake	69
Pigeons	Richard Kell	70
Hedgehog	Anthony Thwaite	72
The Tom-cat	Don Marquis	73
The Hare	John Heath-Stubbs	74
The Tortoise	John Heath-Stubbs	74
Two Performing Elephants	D. H. Lawrence	75
Death of a Fly	Alan Ross	76
The Disclosure	Denise Levertov	76
The Heron	Theodore Roethke	78
The Heron	Phoebe Hesketh	78
The Rabbit (After Prévert)	Alan Brownjohn	79
Creative Writing		81

BALLADS AND STORIES

The Rime of the Ancient Mariner	S. T. Coleridge	83
I Started Early	Emily Dickinson	105

The Sea Serpent Chantey — Vachel Lindsay — 106
Finnegan's Wake — Anon — 108
Casey Jones — Anon — 110

HUMOUR
Tim Turpin — Thomas Hood — 112
Domestic Asides — Thomas Hood — 115
The Two Old Bachelors — Edward Lear — 117
Forth From His Den — Anon — 118
The Hunter — Ogden Nash — 119
The Eel — Ogden Nash — 119
The Termite — Ogden Nash — 119
The Firefly — Ogden Nash — 119
The Young Man of Montrose — Arnold Bennett — 120
There was an old fellow of Tring — Anon — 120
There was an old man from Darjeeling — Anon — 120
There was an old man from Dunoon — Anon — 120
Harvest Hymn — John Betjeman — 121
From *Hiawatha* — H. W. Longfellow — 122
The Modern Hiawatha — Anon — 123
Creative Writing — 124

WEATHER
Rain — Norman Nicholson — 125
Early Rain — James Kirkup — 126
Winter-piece — Charles Tomlinson — 126
Hard Frost — Andrew Young — 127
Fog — Carl Sandburg — 128
Storm in the Black Forest — D. H. Lawrence — 129
The Storm — Theodore Roethke — 129
A Storm — Peter Redgrove — 131
Snow — Andrew Young — 132
A Hot Day — A. S. J. Tessimond — 134
Creative Writing — 134

DREAMS
The Very Image — David Gascoyne — 136
Nightmare — W. S. Gilbert — 137
Kubla Khan — S. T. Coleridge — 141
Portrait of a Boy — Stephen Vincent Benét — 143
The Ice-cart — Wilfrid Gibson — 144
The Nightmare — Wang Yen-Shou (*trans. A. Waley*) — 145

'Who's in The Next Room?'	Thomas Hardy	149
Haunted	Siegfried Sassoon	150
Creative Writing		151
PEOPLE AND PLACES		
Vista	David Gascoyne	153
My Parents Kept Me	Stephen Spender	154
Lollocks	Robert Graves	156
Mole Catcher	Edmund Blunden	160
In a Sailplane	James Kirkup	161
Hunter Trials	John Betjeman	163
I Know Some Lonely Houses off the Road	Emily Dickinson	165
Fishing Harbour Towards Evening	Richard Kell	166
The Bridge	J. Redwood Anderson	167
Morning Glory	Michell Raper	170
Morning at the Window	T. S. Eliot	170
From *Tattooed*	William Plomer	171
The Unfortunate Miller	A. E. Coppard	171
Thrushes	Humbert Wolfe	173
Eight o'Clock	A. E. Housman	174
Roman Wall Blues	W. H. Auden	174
Old Furniture	Thomas Hardy	175
Things Men Have Made	D. H. Lawrence	176
Creative Writing		177
TOWN AND COUNTRY		
Flat Suburbs, S.W., in the Morning	D. H. Lawrence	180
Let Us Be Men	D. H. Lawrence	181
The Manor Farm	Edward Thomas	181
The Beech	Andrew Young	182
Throwing a Tree	Thomas Hardy	183
Root Cellar	Theodore Roethke	184
Digging	Edward Thomas	185
Summer Night	James Kirkup	186
The Winter Trees	Clifford Dyment	186
Creative Writing		188
Index of First Lines		190
Index of Authors		193
Sources and Acknowledgements		194

To the Teacher

The idea of 'teaching poetry' – certainly if the phrase is used in any formal, pedagogic sense – is, in itself, suspect: why, therefore, have we compiled a 'teaching anthology'? Briefly, we felt that there was a need for an anthology which offered more than a collection of poems. Poetry lessons depend so much for their success upon a sympathetic relationship between teacher and pupils and, although books will not in themselves create this relationship, they can help considerably by suggesting ideas for discussion, by showing different approaches to poems, and by encouraging pupils to write poetry themselves. We have attempted to satisfy these needs while avoiding the danger of setting out too rigid a procedure. We hope, too, that the teaching material we include will provide some useful starting-points for teachers looking for fresh ideas.

The pattern of our 'teaching anthology' is as follows. First, in Part A, we introduce three main topics which give information about a particular aspect of poetry, illustrate by examples, point questions and provoke discussion. The individual teacher is the best judge of just how and when to use this area of the book. Secondly, in Part B, we have grouped the material so that the teacher will be able to deal with several poems, linked by some common quality of technique, subject matter, style or attitude, in any one lesson or sequence of lessons. Thirdly, at the end of most sections in Part B, we have provided a number of suggestions for encouraging the pupils to write their own poems, in the belief that it is just as important to get a child to write poetry as it is to encourage him to appreciate and criticise. We consider that it is vital that pupils should be allowed the chance to write, to experiment, to play with words and sounds, even with the shapes of poems in the same way that they are allowed free expression with paints and plastic materials in an art lesson. Through this kind of personal involvement comes an understanding and appreciation of what they read and, above all, an understanding of themselves and the world around them.

Although we do suggest certain lines of thought, we do not wish the books to be followed slavishly as a 'course'. Indeed, the distinction between material suited, for example, to a second as opposed to a first form must sometimes be arbitrary. Although we have numbered our books one to five and have chosen our topics and poems to suit particular age-groups, the teacher will find sufficient flexibility in the arrangement to be able to select and modify the material we print according to his own tastes and the abilities of his pupils.

Creative Writing

There are many ways of stimulating children's writing and every teacher has his own methods. We therefore feel it would be presumptuous to give too much direction and we have in the main limited ourselves to suggestions in the creative writing sections. Whilst we do not positively discourage rhymed verse it is our experience that free verse is the medium best suited to composition at this age. Seeking the correct rhyme and manipulating the words to produce it often kill the original spontaneity and feeling. Free verse enables the child to say what he feels and means and to use the full range of his imagination without being cramped. The approaches to creative writing suggested by M. Langdon* and Sybil Marshall† have, in our experience, worked well and we would encourage teachers using our books to experiment along similar lines with our suggestions for writing poetry. A final word: poems cannot be written on demand and we would emphasise that in using the Creative Writing sections teachers should encourage discussion of our suggestions and not present them to the class as 'exercises' which must be completed.

M. G. B.
P. B.

* Langdon, M. *Let The Children Write: An Explanation Of Intensive Writing* (Longmans)

† Marshall, S. *An Experiment In Education* (C.U.P.)

PART A

SHAPES

The shape of a poem on the page is perhaps the first thing we notice about it and, although we generally give it little attention, it can be most important. The shape of a poem is not an accident, for the writer decides on which line length suits his subject, which of the many forms available to him best expresses his feelings, and he makes the lines work for him.

How do the short lines help the writer in the following poem?

Breathless

(Written at 21,200 feet on May 23rd)

Heart aches,
Lungs pant
The dry air
Sorry, scant.
Legs lift
And why at all?
Loose drift,
Heavy fall.
Prod the snow
Its easiest way;
A flat step
Is holiday.
Look up,
The far stone
Is many miles
Far and alone.

Grind the breath
Once more and on;
Don't look up
Till journey's done.
Must look up,
Glasses are dim.
Wrench of hand
Is breathless limb.
Pause one step,
Breath swings back;
Swallow once,
Dry throat is slack.
Then on
To the far stone;
Don't look up,
Count the steps done.
One step,
One heart-beat,
Stone no nearer
Dragging feet.
Heart aches,
Lungs pant
The dry air
Sorry, scant.

WILFRID NOYCE

Certain words you would normally use if you were writing this description as a composition are missed out.

What sort of words are these and why does the writer omit them?

In your own writing, particularly in free verse, it is very important that you too should make the shape of your poem work for you. If you do not you may find that you have written not a poem but a composition chopped up into short lines. There should always be a reason for the pattern your words make on the page. Do you remember D. H. Lawrence's poem *Bat*? At the moment when he realises that the creatures he is watching are not swallows but bats flying in the gathering gloom, he writes:

Like a glove, a black glove thrown up at the light
And falling back.

Never swallows!
Bats!
The swallows are gone.

At a wavering instant the swallows give way to bats
By the Ponte Vecchio . . .
Changing guard.

Why do the lines take this shape? Why is the one word '*Bats!*' alone on the line? Why the two blank lines?

When you look at the poems *Mountain Lion* on p. 28 and *Mosquito* on p. 25, also by D. H. Lawrence, is the shape of the poem in any way similar to that of *Bat*?

Sometimes writers arrange their poems in such a way that the words actually make an outline picture or recognisable shape on the page, which helps us to see more clearly what is being described. If you turn to p. 32 and p. 35 where you will find two poems, one about Johnny Nolan and the other about a snowflake, you will find that even if you hold the book so far away from you that you cannot read the words you will have some idea of what the poems are about. The shape tells you.

Shape poems may be quite serious, but often the writer works like this because he enjoys playing with words and finds it amusing. Perhaps you already know *The Mouse's Tail* from Lewis Carroll's *Alice's Adventures in Wonderland.*

'Mine is a long and a sad tale,' said the Mouse, turning to Alice, and sighing.

'It *is* a long tail, certainly,' said Alice, looking down with wonder at the Mouse's tail; 'but why do you call it sad?' And she kept on puzzling about it while the Mouse was speaking, so that her idea of the tale was something like this:——'Fury said to

a mouse, That
he met in the
house, "Let
us both go
to law: *I*
will prose-
cute *you*.—
Come, I'll
take no de-
nial: We
must have
the trial;
For really
this morn-
ing I've
nothing
to do."
Said the
mouse to
the cur,
"Such a
trial, dear
sir. With
no jury
or judge,
would
be wast-
ing our
breath."
"I'll be
judge,
I'll be
jury,"
said
cun-
ning
old
Fury:
"I'll
try
the
whole
cause,
and
con-
demn
you to
death".'

Of course this sort of thing upsets the printer, but, when you think about it, there is no reason why poems, particularly those in free verse, should not be more adventurous in shape. The French poet Guillaume Apollinaire wrote a number of short picture-poems called 'calligrams' in which he tried, by the shape of the verse, to illustrate the thing being described. This one was written when he was serving as an artilleryman in the First World War. The poem is in four verses, the last two of which are calligrams. What do the two shapes represent?

Calligram (15th May 1915)

The sky's as blue and black as ink
My eyes drown in it and sink

Darkness a shell whines over me
I write this under a willow tree

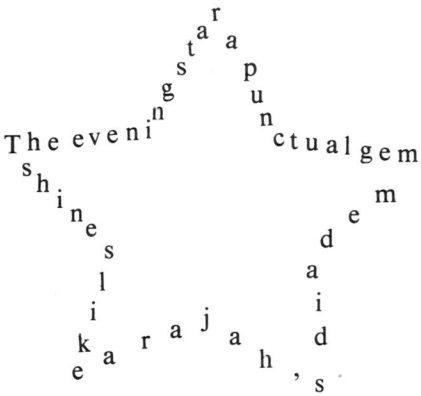

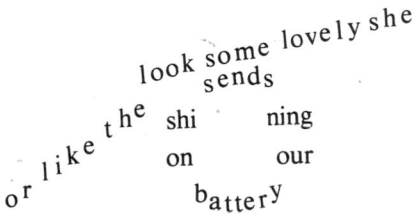

A boy of your own age wrote the following:

I might be a gardener,
I might be a farmer with my shining brand new fork
I might be a murderer

Now write a poem yourself to fit a simple basic shape – a triangle, a diamond, a circle, for example; and then you might like to try something a little more complicated on the lines of the poems above. What words and ideas would fit the shape of a coffin? a church? an eye? a parachute? a fish? a worm? . . . Don't forget that the words and the shape should help each other.

If you need more ideas or examples, look at the Shapes section which begins on p. 25.

SOUNDS

In the last section we saw how the poet can either regard the shape of his poem as an amusing word-game, or as an important device to help the reader understand his meaning – frequently as both. In the same way, the *sounds* of words may be used purely for amusement or, quite seriously, as a means of suggesting a particular feeling or mood. Many of you will already know the following 'nonsense' poem: even if you do, it is worth listening again to its strange sounds and imagining the pictures they conjure up. Notice that the sounds of the words give the poem its 'meaning'. In fact, the sounds of the words often suggest such vivid meanings that one wonders whether 'nonsense' poetry is a fair description.

Jabberwocky

'Twas brillig, and the slithy toves
  Did gyre and gimble in the wabe:
All mimsy were the borogoves,
  And the mome raths outgrabe.

'Beware the Jabberwock, my son!
  The jaws that bite, the claws that catch!
Beware the Jubjub bird, and shun
  The frumious Bandersnatch!'

He took his vorpal sword in hand:
  Long time the manxome foe he sought –
So rested he by the Tumtum tree,
  And stood awhile in thought.

And as in uffish thought he stood,
  The Jabberwock, with eyes of flame,
Came whiffling through the tulgey wood,
  And burbled as it came!

One, two! One, two! And through and through
  The vorpal blade went snicker-snack!
He left it dead, and with its head
  He went galumphing back.

'And hast thou slain the Jabberwock?
  Come to my arms, my beamish boy!
O frabjous day! Callooh! Callay!'
  He chortled in his joy.

'Twas brillig, and the slithy toves
  Did gyre and gimble in the wabe;
All mimsy were the borogoves,
  And the mome raths outgrabe.

LEWIS CARROLL

Lewis Carroll has enjoyed making up new words and new sounds. There is no point in our asking for *precise* definitions of words like 'uffish', 'tulgey', 'brillig' or 'frabjous': they do not have a dictionary meaning. Any meaning they do have for us is what they suggest through their sound.

In Chapter Six of *Through the Looking Glass* Humpty Dumpty explains to Alice the meaning of some of the words. ' "Brillig" ', he says, 'means four o'clock in the afternoon – the time when you begin *broiling* things for dinner', and ' "slithy" means "lithe and slimy" . . . You see it's like a portmanteau* – there are two meanings packed up into one word.' Of course Lewis Carroll's explanations are not necessarily the only ones. Do 'brillig' and 'slithy' suggest something different to you? Discuss the following words and phrases with your teacher. You may decide that some of them are 'portmanteau words', some remind you of real words, and others are simply amusing mixtures of vowels and consonants.

* A trunk in two equal parts for carrying clothes.

toves	gyre and gimble
mimsy	borogoves
mome raths	outgrabe
frumious	vorpal
manxome	uffish
whiffling	tulgey
galumphing	beamish
frabjous	

Why not try some experiments with words yourself? You will find that it can be amusing to invent nonsense words. Try to write a short nonsense poem of your own, but be careful not to use nonsense words *too* freely. Lewis Carroll uses a lot of everyday words as well as those of his own invention. As the subject of your poem you may like to write a sequel to *Jabberwocky*. Look at the second verse again: the Jabberwock is only one of the three possible attackers the boy has to face. Write *your* poem about either the Jubjub bird or the Bandersnatch.

Making up word-sounds is not confined to nonsense poetry as you will see if you look at E. E. Cummings' poems on pp. 30 and 31, G. M. Hopkins' *Inversnaid* on p. 53, or ask yourself what R. Graves means by *Lollocks* on p. 156. In fact every day, all of us use words which represent particular sounds: 'cuckoo', 'hurly-burly', 'croak', 'babble'. These are examples of onomatopœia – which means words like these which attempt to echo the *actual noises* being described. Can you think of any more examples of onomatopœic words?

To help you think more carefully about word-sounds here are two more invented words which you will not find in a dictionary: 'malooma' and 'taketi'.* Which name do you think best describes each shape? Why?

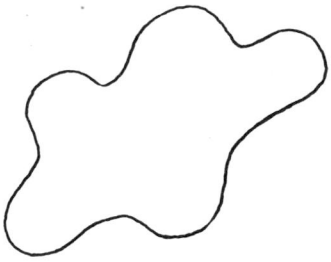

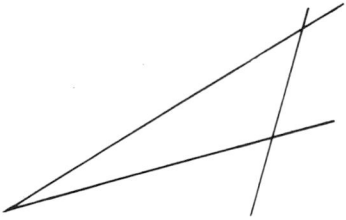

* After Sir F. Bartlett.

Your answers to these questions begin to tell us something about the sounds of the consonants and vowels which make up these words. Here are a dozen words: sort them out into two lists of six – one list for 'maloomas', the other for 'taketis'.

balloon	icicle	snatch
mushroom	oozing	picnic
tripping	summer	puddle
vicious	lash	volume

What sounds have the words in each list in common?

Did you find some words more difficult to classify than others? Why?

Your two lists of words, of course, are only useful to show you clearly how words suggest different qualities by their sounds: these may not only be 'malooma' qualities of bulkiness and puffiness or 'taketi' qualities of sharpness and quickness – but such things as warmth or coldness, lightness or heaviness.

Contrast the sounds of the words in the two extracts which follow. The first describes the death of the two hundred sailors who were the ancient mariner's companions on his horrifying voyage (see p. 83); the second describes some fairy-like spirits.

1 With heavy thump, a lifeless lump,
They dropped down one by one.

2 Transparent forms, too fine for mortal sight,
Their fluid bodies half dissolved in light.
Loose to the wind their airy garments flew,
Thin glittering textures of the filmy dew. . . .

Discuss with your teacher how the *sounds* of the words help to make us see and feel what is being described in each case.

In the next two passages the writers help us to hear the actual sounds of the things they are describing. Listen to this description of doves and bees on a summer's day:

The moan of doves in immemorial elms,
And murmuring of innumerable bees.

Which letters does the writer depend on to create the sounds of the doves and bees?

Listen to this gunfire:

Only the monstrous anger of the guns,
Only the stuttering rifles' rapid rattle
Can patter out their hasty orisons.*

Here, too, the noise is created by the repetition of certain letters – a technique which is given a special name: alliteration. Which letters have been alliterated to produce the sounds of rifle-fire in the extract above? Now have a look at the following extracts: you may want to discuss with your teacher how the sounds fit the subject in each case.

A snake drinking from a water-trough:

He drank enough
And lifted his head, dreamily, as one who has drunken,
And flickered his tongue like a forked night on the air, so black,
Seeming to lick his lips. . . .

A description of autumn:

Season of mists and mellow fruitfulness,
Close bosom-friend of the maturing sun.

A bat flying at twilight:

A circle swoop, a quick parabola under the bridge arches. . . .

Boys skating on a lake and shouting to each other:

So through the darkness and the cold we flew,
And not a voice was idle: with the din
Smitten, the precipices rang aloud;
The leafless trees and every icy crag
Tinkled like iron.

An old wolf:

Lopes on purpose, paddling the snow
Of the soft-blown winterlocked landscape,
Under the loaded branches in the hush of forests.

As some of you will probably have noticed, many of the examples we have used in this section create their particular feelings or moods by their rhythm as much as by their sound: rhythm and movement in poems, therefore, are the next things we must discuss.

* The soldiers' prayers.

RHYTHM AND MOVEMENT

Clap, Clap,
Clap, Clap, Clap,
Clap, Clap, Clap, Clap,
ENGLAND!

Even if you are not an enthusiastic football fan, you will almost certainly have heard this rhythmic chant before and you probably know some similar chants used by supporters of local teams. Perhaps your school or a youth group to which you belong has a war-cry with which supporters urge on their team to victory. If not, you might like to make one up and see if you can give it the impact of the 'England' cry above. First, make sure that your teacher is not of a nervous disposition.

War-cries are as old as mankind and the modern football crowd's rhythmic shouting is often very similar to the chant of warriors preparing for battle against hostile tribes. If you watch travel or adventure films on television you will sometimes see performances of fearsome ritual dances accompanied by rhythmic stamping or shouting and often involving the waving of spears at the most dramatic moments. Rhythm is obviously very important here. Why do people find such chanting helpful and pleasing?

The next poem may help you to answer this question. There are several ways of reading it, but it is probably best if the class is divided into three groups, plus a narrator (or narrator group) for choral speaking. You will need to rehearse and experiment, but if you let the rhythm come through loud and strong you will find that you can build up a dramatic atmosphere.

The Daniel Jazz

Darius the Mede was a king and a wonder.
His eye was proud, and his voice was thunder.
He kept bad lions in a monstrous den.
He fed up the lions on Christian men.

Daniel was the chief hired man of the land.
He stirred up the jazz in the palace band.
He whitewashed the cellar, he shovelled in the coal;
And Daniel kept a-praying, 'Lord, save my soul.'
Daniel kept a-praying, 'Lord, save my soul!'
Daniel kept a-praying, 'Lord, save my soul!'

Daniel was the butler, swagger and swell.
He ran up stairs. He answered the bell.
And *he* would let in whoever came a-calling –
Saints so holy, scamps so appalling.
Old man Ahab leaves his card.
Elisha and the bears are a-waiting in the yard.
Here comes Pharaoh and his snakes a-calling.
Here comes Cain and his wife a-calling.
Shadrach, Meshach and Abednego for tea.
Here comes Jonah, and the Whale,
And the *Sea!*
Here comes St. Peter and his fishing pole.
Here comes Judas and his silver a-calling.
Here comes old Beelzebub a-calling.
And Daniel kept a-praying, 'Lord, save my soul!'
Daniel kept a-praying, 'Lord, save my soul!'
Daniel kept a-praying, 'Lord, save my soul!'

His sweetheart and his mother were Christian and meek.
They washed and ironed for Darius every week.
One Thursday he met them at the door:
Paid them as usual, but acted sore.

He said, 'Your Daniel is a dead little pigeon.
He's a good hard worker, but he talks religion.'
And he showed them Daniel in the lions' cage;
Daniel standing quietly, the lions in a rage.
His good old mother cried, 'Lord, save him!'
And Daniel's tender sweetheart cried, 'Lord, save him!'

And she was a golden lily in the dew,
And she was as sweet as an apple on the tree,
And she was as fine as a melon in the corn-field,
Gliding and lovely as a ship on the sea,
Gliding and lovely as a ship on the sea.
And she prayed to the Lord:
'Send Gabriel. Send Gabriel.'

King Darius said to the lions:
'Bite Daniel. Bite Daniel.
Bite him. Bite him. Bite him!'

Thus roared the lions:
'We want Daniel, Daniel, Daniel,
We want Daniel, Daniel, Daniel.
Grrrrrrrrrrrrrrrrrrrrrrrrrrrrrrrrrrrrrrrr
Grrrrrrrrrrrrrrrrrrrrrrrrrrrrrrrrrrrrrrrr.'

And Daniel did not frown,
Daniel did not cry;
He kept on looking at the sky.
And the Lord said to Gabriel:
'Go chain the lions down.
Go chain the lions down.
Go chain the lions down.'

And Gabriel chained the lions,
And Gabriel chained the lions,
And Gabriel chained the lions,
And Daniel got out of the den,
And Daniel got out of the den,
And Daniel got out of the den.

And Darius said, 'You're a Christian child.'
Darius said, 'You're a Christian child.'
Darius said, 'You're a Christian child.'
And gave him his job again,
And gave him his job again,
And gave him his job again.

VACHEL LINDSAY

People like rhythm: it is part of them from the moment they are born. There are the minute personal rhythms of the heartbeat, pulse and breathing; the natural rhythm of our daily routine – sleeping, eating, washing, playing – which become part of the larger rhythms of time such as day following day and weeks turning into months and years. There is the rhythm of the day as light follows darkness only to be plunged into darkness again; the rhythm of the year as winter gives way to spring and summer to autumn and for all living things the rhythms of birth, life and death. Very often, people spend much of their lives working at tasks involving repetitive movements and they sometimes develop rhythmic songs to help them in their work. Children, also, like rhythmic songs ranging from nursery rhymes to the chants that they make up when playing. Tony Connor's poem on p. 58 may remind you of some of these. Can you think of any more examples of work or play songs?

We enjoy rhythms of all kinds, particularly the rhythms of tunes which we find 'catchy'. Why, by the way, do we use this word 'catchy'? Sometimes, almost without realising, we tap our feet to the rhythm. A good dance rhythm makes us want to *move* rhythmically, to be a part of the music ourselves. If you watch people dancing, you will often see that their faces show that they have been completely taken over by the music, almost as if they have escaped into another world. Watch the player on the drums or the bass and you will see that he is generally allowed very little rest, for it is he who provides the basic beat of the music and, very often, holds the whole piece together. What current pop songs rely on a strong beat for much of their effect?

As in music, rhythm in poetry is a kind of pattern which underlies the whole structure. Occasionally, as in some kinds of music, the rhythm may be so strong that it is the most important part of the poem; sometimes it is quiet and almost unnoticed. Ideally it helps the subject being described. How does it help here?

Night Mail

This is the night mail crossing the border,
Bringing the cheque and the postal order,
Letters for the rich, letters for the poor,
The shop at the corner and the girl next door.
Pulling up Beattock, a steady climb –
The gradient's against her, but she's on time.

Past cotton grass and moorland boulder
Shovelling white steam over her shoulder,
Snorting noisily as she passes
Silent miles of wind-bent grasses.
Birds turn their heads as she approaches,
Stare from the bushes at her blank-faced coaches.
Sheep dogs cannot turn her course,
They slumber on with paws across.
In the farm she passes no-one wakes,
But a jug in the bedroom gently shakes.

Dawn freshens, the climb is done.
Down towards Glasgow she descends
Towards the steam tugs yelping down the glade of cranes,
Towards the fields of apparatus, the furnaces
Set on the dark plain like gigantic chessmen.
All Scotland waits for her:
In the dark glens, beside the pale-green lochs,
Men long for news.

Letters of thanks, letters from banks,
Letters of joy from girl and boy,
Receipted bills and invitations
To inspect new stock or visit relations,
And applications for situations
And timid lovers' declarations
And gossip, gossip from all the nations,
News circumstantial, news financial,
Letters with holiday snaps to enlarge in,
Letters with faces scrawled in the margin,

Letters from uncles, cousins and aunts,
Letters to Scotland from the South of France,
Letters of condolence to Highlands and Lowlands,
Notes from overseas to Hebrides –
Written on paper of every hue,
The pink, the violet, the white and the blue,
The chatty, the catty, the boring, adoring,
The cold and official and the heart's outpouring,
Clever, stupid, short and long,
The typed and the printed and the spelt all wrong.

Thousands are still asleep
Dreaming of terrifying monsters,
Or a friendly tea beside the band at Cranston's or Crawford's.
Asleep in working Glasgow, asleep in well-set Edinburgh,
Asleep in granite Aberdeen.
They continue their dreams;
But shall wake soon and long for letters,
And none will hear the postman's knock
Without a quickening of the heart,
For who can hear and feel himself forgotten?

W. H. AUDEN

How does the rhythm of the poem vary from verse to verse? Why is this?

Rhythm does not necessarily have to be *regular* – it may vary with our feelings or our mood. Try saying the following sentence in two or three different moods – sadly, happily, angrily, enviously:

'John has a brand new bicycle'

Each time the rhythm is different because our varying moods give a slightly different emphasis to the pattern of words.

Poems have irregular rhythms too. Look at this description of the sound of church bells from the beginning of D. H. Lawrence's poem, *Weeknight Service.*

The five old bells
Are hurrying and stridently calling,
Insisting, protesting

They are right, yet clamorously falling
Into gabbling confusion, without resting,
Like spattering shouts of an orator endlessly dropping
From the tower on the town, but endlessly, never stopping.

How does the rhythm of the lines help us to imagine the bells? There is one sort of word which is used many times here to create rhythm (and noise!). What is it?

Here is another passage which has a different type of irregular rhythm.

Here at the small field's ending pause
Where the chalk wall falls to the foam and its tall ledges
Oppose the pluck
And knock of the tide,
And the shingle scrambles after the suck-
ing surf, and the gull lodges
A moment on its sheer side.

W. H. AUDEN (from *Look, Stranger*)

How would you describe the rhythm of this piece and how does it suit the subject?

All poems have some sort of rhythm which, as you can see from the examples we have looked at, depends on several things: the choice of words, the sounds these words make, the order in which they are written, and the shape of poem the poet uses. In some cases 'rhythm' is perhaps not the best word to describe what we are talking about and, particularly in the last example, 'movement' is sometimes a more suitable word.

PART B

SHAPES

The Mosquito

When did you start your tricks
Monsieur?

What do you stand on such high legs for?
Why this length of shredded shank
You exaltation?

Is it that you shall lift your centre of gravity upwards
And weigh no more than air as you alight upon me,
Stand upon me weightless, you phantom?

I heard a woman call you the Winged Victory
In sluggish Venice.
You turn your head towards your tail, and smile.

How can you put so much devilry
Into that translucent phantom shred
Of a frail corpus?

Queer, with your thin wings and your streaming legs
How you sail like a heron, or a dull clot of air,
A nothingness.

Yet what an aura surrounds you;
Your evil little aura, prowling, and casting a numbness on
my mind.

That is your trick, your bit of filthy magic:
Invisibility, and the anaesthetic power
To deaden my attention in your direction.

But I know your game now, streaky sorcerer.

Queer, how you stalk and prowl the air
In circles and evasions, enveloping me,
Ghoul on wings
Winged Victory.

Settle, and stand on long thin shanks
Eyeing me sideways, and cunningly conscious that I am
  aware,
You speck.

I hate the way you lurch off sideways into air
Having read my thoughts against you.

Come then, let us play at unawares,
And see who wins in this sly game of bluff.
Man or mosquito.

You don't know that I exist, and I don't know that you exist.
Now then!

It is your trump
It is your hateful little trump
You pointed fiend,
Which shakes my sudden blood to hatred of you:
It is your small, high, hateful bugle in my ear.

Why do you do it?
Surely it is bad policy.

They say you can't help it.
If that is so, then I believe a little in Providence protecting
the innocent.
But it sounds so amazingly like a slogan
A yell of triumph as you snatch my scalp.

Blood, red blood
Super-magical
Forbidden liquor.

I behold you stand
For a second enspasmed in oblivion,
Obscenely ecstasied
Sucking live blood
My blood.

Such silence, such suspended transport,
Such gorging,
Such obscenity of trespass.

You stagger
As well as you may.
Only your accursed hairy frailty
Your own imponderable weightlessness
Saves you, wafts you away on the very draught my anger
makes in its snatching.

Away with a paean of derision
You winged blood-drop.

Can I not overtake you?
Are you one too many for me
Winged Victory?
Am I not mosquito enough to out-mosquito you?

Queer, what a big stain my sucked blood makes
Beside the infinitesimal faint smear of you!
Queer, what a dim dark smudge you have disappeared into!

D. H. LAWRENCE

Mountain Lion

Climbing through the January snow, into the Lobo canyon
Dark grow the spruce-trees, blue is the balsam, water sounds
still unfrozen, and the trail is still evident.

Men!
Two men!
Men! The only animal in the world to fear!

They hesitate.
We hesitate.
They have a gun.
We have no gun.

Then we all advance, to meet.

Two Mexicans, strangers, emerging out of the dark and snow
and inwardness of the Lobo valley.
What are you doing here on this vanishing trail?

What is he carrying?
Something yellow.
A deer?

Que tiene, amigo?
Leon –

He smiles, foolishly, as if he were caught doing wrong.
And we smile, foolishly, as if we didn't know.
He is quite gentle and dark-faced.

It is a mountain lion,
A long, long slim cat, yellow like a lioness.
Dead.
He trapped her this morning, he says, smiling foolishly.

Lift up her face,
Her round, bright face, bright as frost.
Her round, fine-fashioned head, with two dead ears;
And stripes in the brilliant frost of her face, sharp, fine dark rays,
Dark, keen, fine eyes in the brilliant frost of her face.
Beautiful dead eyes.

Hermoso es!

They go out towards the open;
We go on into the gloom of Lobo.
And above the trees I found her lair,
A hole in the blood-orange brilliant rocks that stick up, a little cave,
And bones, and twigs, and a perilous ascent.

So, she will never leap up that way again, with the yellow flash of a mountain lion's long shoot!
And her bright striped frost-face will never watch any more, out of the shadow of the cave in the blood-orange rock,
Above the trees of the Lobo dark valley-mouth!

Instead, I look out.
And out to the dim of the desert, like a dream, never real;

To the snow of the Sangre de Cristo mountains, the ice of the mountains of Picoris,
And near across at the opposite steep of snow, green trees motionless standing in snow, like a Christmas toy.

And I think in this empty world there was room for me and a mountain lion.
And I think in the world beyond, how easily we might spare a million or two of humans
And never miss them.
Yet what a gap in the world, the missing white frost-face of that slim yellow mountain lion!

D. H. LAWRENCE

insu nli gh t

o
verand
o
vering

A

onc
eup
ona
tim

e ne wsp aper

e. e. cummings

one

t
hi
s

snowflake

(a
  li
    ght
  in
g)

is upon a gra

v
es
t

one

e. e. cummings

To a Snowflake

What heart could have thought you? –
Past our devisal
(O filigree petal!)
Fashioned so purely,
Fragilely, surely,
From what Paradisal
Imagineless metal,
Too costly for cost?
Who hammered you, wrought you,
From argentine vapour? –
'God was my shaper.
Passing surmisal,
He hammered, He wrought me,
From curled silver vapour,
To lust of His mind: –
Thou couldst not have thought me!
So purely, so palely,
Tinily, surely,
Mightily, frailly,
Insculpted and embossed,
With His hammer of wind,
And His graver of frost.'

FRANCIS THOMPSON

in Just –
spring when the world is mud –
luscious the little
lame balloonman

whistles far and wee

and eddieandbill come
running from marbles and
piracies and it's
spring

when the world is puddle-wonderful

the queer
old balloonman whistles
far and wee
and bettyandisabel come dancing

from hop-scotch and jump-rope and

it's
spring
and
    the

        goat-footed

balloonMan whistles
far
and
wee

e. e. cummings

From The Gecko

(For J. P.)

I don't know how many thousand years
Of evolution have not taught the gecko
You can't jump *up* downwards.

Blue-flecked, pink-flecked, semi-transparent,
Sucker-footed, he creeps
Across the ceiling. He sees
With his extraordinary protuberant eyes
A fly, just hovering below him . . . He
                jumps
                and
Flick!
    He falls to the floor:
Poor little half-dazed lizard!

JOHN HEATH-STUBBS

Johnny Nolan

Johnny Nolan has a patch on his ass

Kids chase him
thru screendoor summers
Thru the back streets
of all my memories
Somewhere a man laments
upon a violin
A doorstep baby cries
and cries again
like
a
ball
bounced
down steps
Which helps the afternoon arise again
To a moment of remembered hysteria

Johnny Nolan has a patch on his ass

Kids chase him

LAWRENCE FERLINGHETTI

The Computer's First Christmas Card

jollymerry
hollyberry
jollyberry
merryholly
happyjolly
jollyjelly
jellybelly
bellymerry
hollyheppy
jollyMolly
marryJerry
merryHarry
hoppyBarry
heppyJarry
boppyheppy
berryjorry
jorryjolly
moppyjelly
Mollymerry
Jerryjolly
bellyboppy
jorryhoppy
hollymoppy
Barrymerry
Jarryhappy
happyboppy
boppyjolly
jollymerry
merrymerry
merrymerry
merryChris
ammerryasa
Chrismerry
asMERRYCHR
YSANTHEMUM

EDWIN MORGAN

On This Island

Look, stranger, at this island now
The leaping light for your delight discovers,
Stand stable here
And silent be,
That through the channels of the ear
May wander like a river
The swaying sound of the sea.

Here at the small field's ending pause
Where the chalk wall falls to the foam, and its tall ledges
Oppose the pluck
And knock of the tide,
And the shingle scrambles after the suck-
ing surf, and the gull lodges
A moment on its sheer side.

Far off like floating seeds the ships
Diverge on urgent voluntary errands;
And the full view
Indeed may enter
And move in memory as now these clouds do,
That pass the harbour mirror
And all the summer through the water saunter.

W. H. AUDEN

Creative Writing

1 If you choose to write about any of the following subjects, concentrate particularly on their outlines: a rocket (the photograph on p. 39 might help); a church spire; a factory chimney; an axe or a flag; a globe; a raindrop; a staircase; a pillar-box; a windmill; a sea-shell; a leaf; a spiral – it could be a spring, a staircase or a helter-skelter.

There are several ways in which you can help yourself to see the shapes of things. You could, for example, imagine them as silhouettes and write a poem which fills the black area, or you could simply make your words follow the outline of the shape as Apollinaire does in his *Calligram* on p. 7.

2 Look at the photograph of the Forth bridges on p. 20. The new bridge in the foreground is obviously constructed in a quite different way from the old one beyond it. Here, as everywhere else, bridges vary according to the materials of which they are made, the job they have to do, and the time at which they were built; but they have one thing in common – a clearly defined shape. There are, of course, many more types of bridge – hump-back bridges, motorway bridges, bridges that open, railway viaducts, and so on – you can probably think of some in your own area. Using either the photograph or bridges that you already know, write a poem about bridges. You can, if you wish, concentrate entirely on the shape in one of the ways outlined in the suggestion above.

3 In *Breathless* on p. 3 Wilfrid Noyce uses the shape of the poem both to emphasise the strain felt by the climber and also to convey the idea of a high mountain. Try to write your own poem based on the idea of descent rather than ascent. You may, for example, imagine yourself as a deep-sea diver being lowered into the depths of the ocean; as a pot-holer worming his way deeper into the earth; or (rather more rapid these), as a swimmer diving or jumping from a high board, or a passenger in a descending lift. Whichever subject you choose you may find it useful to shape your poem in a similar way to *Breathless.*

4 In E. E. Cummings' poem on p. 31 notice how the words are arranged on the page to suggest the lazy, indirect fall of a snowflake. You may be able to think of other things – falling leaves, a feather drifting to the ground, a sky-rocket on November 5th, soaring and bursting as it falls – which you could write about in a similar way.

5 *The Computer's First Christmas Card* on p. 36 may suggest to you other ideas for poems written by computer. How do you imagine a computer might greet someone? say goodbye? finish a letter? How might it describe frog-spawn? a penny-farthing bicycle? a schoolteacher?

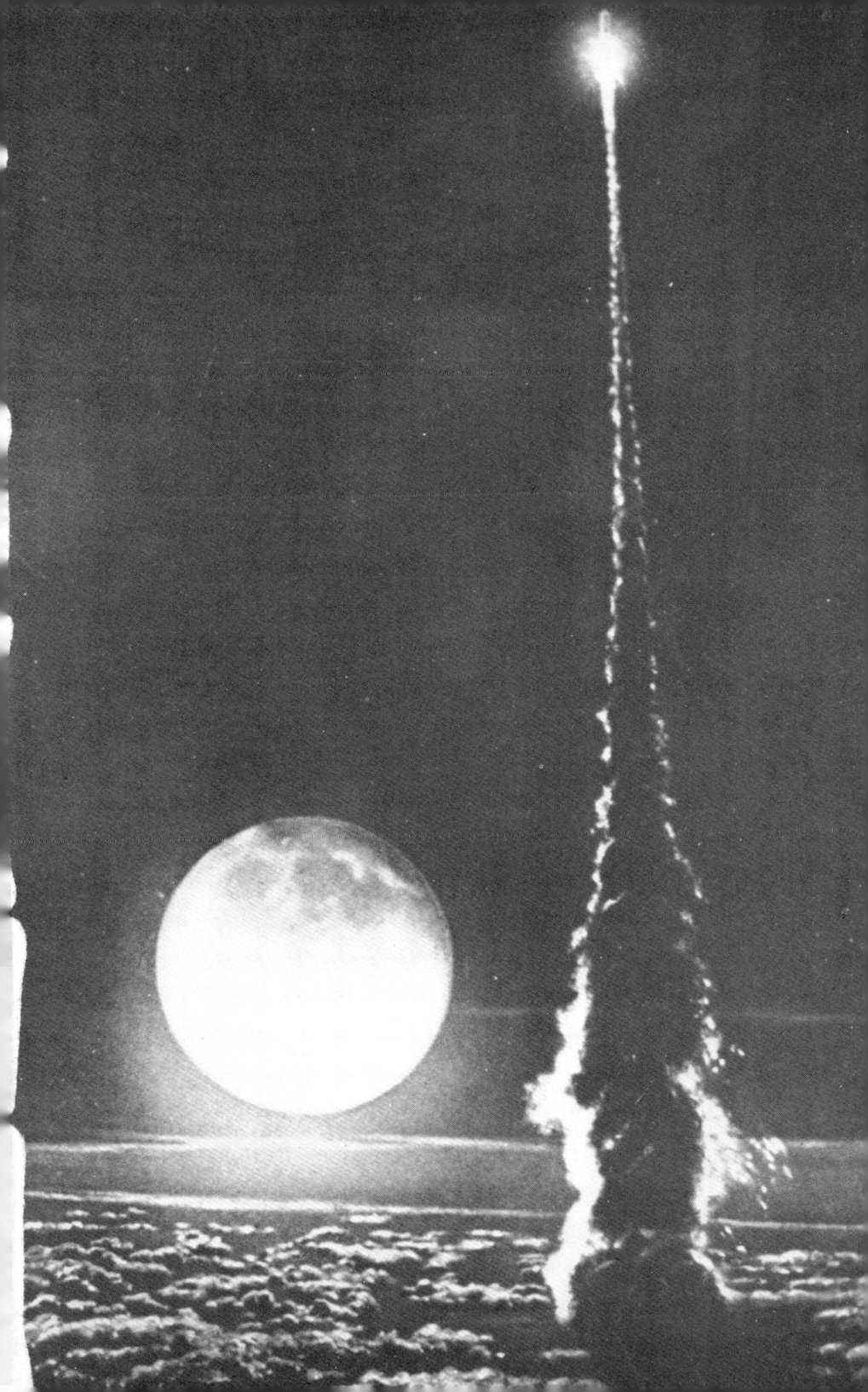

SOUNDS

Thunder and Lightning*

Blood punches through every vein
As lightning strips the windowpane.

Under its flashing whip, a white
Village leaps to light.

On tubs of thunder, fists of rain
Slog it out of sight again.

Blood punches the heart with fright
As rain belts the village night.

JAMES KIRKUP

* You will find other poems about storms in the Weather section.

From Fall of a Tower

The Town is

Still

Then

Over the Town there came a rumble
The Church's
Great columns starting to mumble

The sound was swelling, growing louder,
The stone-hung pillars shook, stumbling
Inwards, then broke with booming sag.

The Tower with a snarl
Flung its tongues into jangle –
Monsoon marching in hot hate through jungle.

The sound moved into roar, then from the roar
Leapt out a tearing screech, when
Apse, aching apart,
Sped into careering halves, and

With a maddened snarl
The Tower
Flung its tongues into
Chords of an iron alarm
Lashing them to jangle.

The roar bursts into thunder and
Tower, rocking, flays
Itself from side to side with lurch
That drums out grunts, and

To a boom of rollers
Shakes its drunken bulk. Then, with a crack,
Roof-rafters fly, sweep round jagged stumps
Under their riding tower. Pinnacles awag
In anger flourish; then in typhoon howl
Gargoyles leap from posterns
Pell-mell, grunt into earth.

Struts straddle; West Front
Walks apart, begins ungainly waddle,
Collapses on its face; brick and mortar
Flee yelling from their stocks; huge blocks
Jerk bounding parabolas, booming
Tomb-slabs throw sepulchral cart-wheels;
Roof rives asunder, and in gasps
Buttresses fall flat.
The Tower
Rolls rolls from side to side, but in explosion

Supports creak apart, mullions moaning
Yawn and, with a last agony crash of iron,
The Tower falls
And floods the ground in ruins.

FRANCIS BERRY

The Blacksmiths

Swart, swarthy smiths besmattered with smoke
Drive me to death with the din of their dints.
Such noise on nights heard no one never;
What knavish cry and clattering of knocks!
The snub-nosed changelings cry after 'Coal! Coal!'
And blow their bellows till all their brains burst:
'Huff, puff!' pants one; 'Haff, paff!' another.
They spit and sprawl and spin many yarns;
They grind teeth and gnash them, and groan together,
Hot with the heaving of their hard hammers.
Aprons they have of hide of the bull.
Their shanks are shielded from the fierce sparks:
Heavy hammers they have, that are hard handled;
Stark strokes they strike on an anvil of steel.
Lus, bus! Las, das! they strike in rotation:
The Devil destroy such a doleful din.
The master lengthens a little piece, belabours a smaller,
Twines the two together, and strikes a treble note
Tik, tak! Hic, hac! Tiket, taket! Tik, tak!
Lus, bus! Las, das! such lives they lead
All horseshoers; Christ give them sorrow
For none for these water burners at night may rest

ANON

Elinour Rumming

Tell you I chyll*, *will*
If that ye will
A while be still,
Of a comely gill
That dwelt on a hill:
But she is not gryll*, *fierce*
For she is somewhat sage
And well worn in age;
For her visage
It would assuage
A man's courage.
  Her loathly lere
Is nothing clear,
But ugly of cheer,
Droopy and drowsy,
Scurvy and lousy;
Her face all bowsy,
Comely crinkled,
Wondersly wrinkled,
Like a roast pig's ear,
Bristled with hair.
  Her lewd lips twain,
They slaver, men sayne,
Like a ropy rain,
A gummy glare:
She is ugly fair;
Her nose somdele* hookèd, *somewhat*
And camously crooked,
Never stopping,
But ever dropping;
Her skin loose and slack,
Grained like a sack;
With a crooked back.

Her huke* of Lincoln green, *cloak*
It had been hers, I ween,
More than forty year;
And so it doth appear,
For the green bare threads
Look like sere weeds,
Withered like hay,
The wool worn away;
And yet I dare say
She thinketh herself gay
Upon the holy day,
When she doth her array
And girdeth in her geets* *clothes*
Stitched and pranked with pleats,
Her kirtle Bristol-red,
With clothes upon her head
That weigh a sow* of lead, *large block*
Writhen in wonder wise,
After the Saracens' guise,
With a whim wham,
Knit with a trim tram
Upon her brain pan,
Like an Egyptian* *gypsy*
Cappèd about:
When she goeth out
Herself for to show,
She driveth down the dew
With a pair of heels
As broad as two wheels;
She hobbles as a goose
With her blanket hose
Over the fallow;
Her shoon smeared with tallow,
Greased upon dirt
That baudeth her skirt.

And this comely dame,
I understand her name,
Is Elinour Rumming, . . .

JOHN SKELTON

Jazz Fantasia

Drum on your drums, batter on your banjoes,
sob on the long cool winding saxophones.
Go to it, O jazzmen.

Sling your knuckles on the bottoms of the happy
tin pans, let your trombones ooze, and go husha-
husha-hush with the slippery sandpaper.

Moan like an autumn wind high in the lonesome treetops, moan soft like
you wanted somebody terrible, cry like a racing car slipping away from a
motorcycle cop, bang-bang! you jazzmen, bang altogether drums, traps,
banjoes, horns, tin cans – make two people fight on the top of a stairway
and scratch each other's eyes in a cinch tumbling down the stairs.

Can the rough stuff . . . now a Mississippi steamboat pushes up the night
river with a hoo-hoo-hoo-oo . . . and the green lanterns calling to the high
soft stars . . . a red moon rides on the humps of the low river hills . . .
go to it, O jazzmen.

CARL SANDBURG

Silences

There is the silence of a copse or croft
    When the wind sinks dumb,
    And of belfry-loft
When the tenor after tolling stops its hum.

And there's the silence of a lonely pond
    Where a man was drowned,
    Nor nigh nor yond
A newt, frog, toad, to make the merest sound.

But the rapt silence of an empty house
    Where oneself was born,
    Dwelt, held carouse
With friends, is of all silences most forlorn!

Past are remembered songs and music-strains
    Once audible there:
    Roof, rafters, panes
Look absent-thoughted, tranced, or locked in prayer.

It seems no power on earth can waken it
    Or rouse its rooms,
    Or its past permit
The present to stir a torpor like a tomb's.

THOMAS HARDY

Echo

'Who called?' I said, and the words
  Through the whispering glades,
Hither, thither, baffled the birds –
  'Who called? Who called?'

The leafy boughs on high
  Hissed in the sun;
The dark air carried my cry
  Faintingly on:

Eyes in the green, in the shade,
  In the motionless brake,
Voices that said what I said,
  For mockery's sake:

'Who cares?' I bawled through my tears;
  The wind fell low:
In the silence, 'Who cares? Who cares?'
  Wailed to and fro.

WALTER DE LA MARE

The Splendour Falls

  The splendour falls on castle walls
    And snowy summits old in story:
  The long light shakes across the lakes,
    And the wild cataract leaps in glory.
Blow, bugle, blow, set the wild echoes flying,
Blow, bugle; answer, echoes, dying, dying, dying.

O hark. O hear! how thin and clear,
And thinner, clearer, farther going!
O sweet and far from cliff and scar
The horns of Elfland faintly blowing!
Blow, let us hear the purple glens replying:
Blow, bugle; answer, echoes, dying, dying, dying.

O love, they die in yon rich sky,
They faint on hill or field or river:
Our echoes roll from soul to soul,
And grow for ever and for ever.
Blow, bugle, blow, set the wild echoes flying,
And answer, echoes, answer, dying, dying, dying.

LORD TENNYSON

Pleasant Sounds

The rustling of leaves under the feet in woods and under hedges;
The crumping of cat-ice and snow down wood-rides, narrow lanes and every street causeway;
Rustling through a wood or rather rushing, while the wind halloos in the oak-top like thunder;
The rustle of birds' wings startled from their nests or flying unseen into the bushes;
The whizzing of larger birds overhead in a wood, such as crows, paddocks*, buzzards; *kites*
The trample of robins and woodlarks on the brown leaves, and the patter of squirrels on the green moss;
The fall of an acorn on the ground, the pattering of nuts on the hazel branches as they fall from ripeness;
The flirt of ground-lark's wing from the stubbles – how sweet such pictures on dewy mornings, when the dew flashes from its brown feathers!

JOHN CLARE

Creative Writing

1 Write down as many comparisons as you can which are suggested by the following sounds:
a ship's hooter or fog-horn;
the roar of a crowd at a football match;
applause;
distant thunder;
the wind in the trees;
the noise of a waterfall – the Niagara picture above should help you.

2 Perhaps you remember how Lewis Carroll invented 'nonsense' words in his poem *Jabberwocky* (p. 9). Now try to make up your own nonsense words to suggest the sound and feeling of the following:

The first helping of blancmange being spooned out of a large bowl
Fingernails or chalk scraping down a blackboard
Bathwater going down the plughole
A learner-driver crashing the gears of a car

3 Jot down quickly a list of sounds that you like and another of sounds you dislike. For example, you may enjoy the crackle of sweet-papers, but quail at the sound of the dentist's drill. When you have made your lists you may want to use these notes to write a poem contrasting your likes and dislikes.

Try to make the sounds real for the reader – perhaps by using comparisons (as in 1 on p. 51) or by inventing words to suggest the noise you want (as in 2).

4 A time when most people are particularly aware of sounds is when they are lying in bed in the morning and can hear but not see the things going on around them – the milkman on his round . . . noises from the kitchen . . . the paper-boy . . . a neighbour setting off to work . . .

You may be able to write a poem which describes this time of day in and around your own home.

5 As you will realise from the previous suggestion, we are much more conscious of sounds when we cannot see what is causing them. A blind person must be particularly sensitive to noises. Imagine yourself to be either in a busy street, or in a large and crowded department store, or in the school dining-hall at lunch time. Close your eyes and concentrate on the sounds. If you have really imagined the scene clearly you should be able to write down your impressions.

RHYTHM AND MOVEMENT

Inversnaid

This darksome burn, horseback brown,
His rollrock highroad roaring down,
In coop and in comb the fleece of his foam
Flutes and low to the lake falls home.

A wind-puff bonnet of fáwn-fróth
Turns and twindles over the broth
Of a pool so pitchblack, féll-frówning,
It rounds and rounds Despair to drowning.

Degged with dew, dappled with dew
Are the groins of the braes that the brook treads through,
Wiry heathpacks, flitches of fern,
And the beadbonny ash that sits over the burn.

What would the world be, once bereft
Of wet and of wildness? Let them be left,
O let them be left, wildness and wet;
Long live the weeds and the wilderness yet.

G. M. HOPKINS

The Quarry

O what is that sound which so thrills the ear
  Down in the valley drumming, drumming?
Only the scarlet soldiers, dear,
  The soldiers coming.

O what is that light I see flashing so clear
  Over the distance brightly, brightly?
Only the sun on their weapons, dear,
  As they step lightly.

O what are they doing with all that gear,
  What are they doing this morning, this morning?
Only their usual manoeuvres, dear,
  Or perhaps a warning.

O why have they left the road down there,
  Why are they suddenly wheeling, wheeling?
Perhaps a change in their orders, dear,
  Why are you kneeling?

O haven't they stopped for the doctor's care,
  Haven't they reined their horses, their horses?
Why they are none of them wounded, dear,
  None of these forces.

O is it the parson they want, with white hair,
  Is it the parson, is it, is it?
No, they are passing his gateway, dear,
  Without a visit.

O it must be the farmer who lives so near.
  It must be the farmer so cunning, so cunning?
They have passed the farmyard already, dear,
  And now they are running.

O where are you going? Stay with me here!
  Were the vows you swore deceiving, deceiving?
No, I promised to love you, dear,
  But I must be leaving.

O it's broken the lock and splintered the door,
  O it's the gate where they're turning, turning
Their boots are heavy on the floor
  And their eyes are burning.

W. H. AUDEN

Tarantella

Do you remember an Inn,
Miranda?
Do you remember an Inn?
And the tedding and the spreading
Of the straw for a bedding,
And the fleas that tease in the High Pyrenees,
And the wine that tasted of the tar?
And the cheers and the jeers of the young muleteers
(Under the vine of the dark verandah)?
Do you remember an Inn, Miranda,
Do you remember an Inn?
And the cheers and the jeers of the young muleteers
Who hadn't got a penny,
And who weren't paying any,
And the hammer at the doors and the Din?
And the Hip! Hop! Hap!
Of the clap
Of the hands to the twirl and the swirl
Of the girl gone chancing,
Glancing,
Dancing,
Backing and advancing,
Snapping of a clapper to the spin
Out and in –
And the Ting, Tong, Tang of the Guitar!
Do you remember an Inn,
Miranda?
Do you remember an Inn?

Never more;
Miranda,
Never more.
Only the high peaks hoar:
And Aragon a torrent at the door.
No sound
In the walls of the Halls where falls
The tread
Of the feet of the dead to the ground
No sound:
But the boom
Of the far Waterfall like Doom.

HILAIRE BELLOC

Skimbleshanks: The Railway Cat

There's a whisper down the line at 11.39
When the Night Mail's ready to depart,
Saying 'Skimble where is Skimble has he gone to hunt the
  thimble?
We must find him or the train can't start.'
All the guards and all the porters and the stationmaster's
  daughters
They are searching high and low,
Saying 'Skimble where is Skimble for unless he's very nimble
Then the Night Mail just can't go.'
At 11.42 when the signal's nearly due
And the passengers are frantic to a man –
Then Skimble will appear and he'll saunter to the rear:
He's been busy in the luggage van!
    He gives one flash of his glass-green eyes
      And the signal goes 'All Clear!'
    And we're off at last for the northern part
      Of the Northern Hemisphere!

You may say that by and large it is Skimble who's in charge
Of the Sleeping Car Express.
From the driver and the guards to the bagmen playing cards
He will supervise them all, more or less.
Down the corridor he paces and examines all the faces
Of the travellers in the First and in the Third;
He establishes control by a regular patrol
And he'd know at once if anything occurred.
He will watch you without winking and he sees what you are thinking
And it's certain that he doesn't approve
Of hilarity and riot, so the folk are very quiet
When Skimble is about and on the move.
You can play no pranks with Skimbleshanks!
He's a Cat that cannot be ignored;
So nothing goes wrong on the Northern Mail
When Skimbleshanks is aboard.

Oh it's very pleasant when you have found your little den
With your name written up on the door.
And the berth is very neat with a newly folded sheet
And there's not a speck of dust on the floor.
There is every sort of light – you can make it dark or bright;
There's a handle that you turn to make a breeze.
There's a funny little basin you're supposed to wash your face in
And a crank to shut the window if you sneeze.
Then the guard looks in politely and will ask you very brightly
'Do you like your morning tea weak or strong?'
But Skimble's just behind him and was ready to remind him,
For Skimble won't let anything go wrong.
And when you creep into your cosy berth
And pull up the counterpane,
You ought to reflect that it's very nice
To know that you won't be bothered by mice –
You can leave all that to the Railway Cat,
The Cat of the Railway Train !

In the watches of the night he is always fresh and bright;
Every now and then he has a cup of tea
With perhaps a drop of Scotch while he's keeping on the
watch,
Only stopping here and there to catch a flea.
You were fast asleep at Crewe and so you never knew
That he was walking up and down the station;
You were sleeping all the while he was busy at Carlisle,
Where he greets the stationmaster with elation.
But you saw him at Dumfries, where he speaks to the police
If there's anything they ought to know about:
When you get to Gallowgate there you do not have to wait –
For Skimbleshanks will help you to get out!
He gives you a wave of his long brown tail
Which says: 'I'll see you again!
You'll meet without fail on the Midnight Mail
The Cat of the Railway Train.'

T. S. ELIOT

Child's Bouncing Song

Molly Vickers
wets her knickers,
Georgie's father's big and black,
cream on Sunday
milk on Monday,
I'm the cock of all the back.

Tell me who's a
bigger boozer
Mister Baker beats them all,
from his lorry
watch him hurry,
touch the ground and touch the wall.

Who're the gentry
down our entry –
Mrs. Smith's got two T.V.'s.
What if her coat
is a fur coat,
all her kids are full of fleas.

Joan loves Harry,
Jack will marry
Edna when they both grow up,
I'll announce it,
bounce bounce bounce it,
our dog Whisker's had a pup.

High and low and
to and fro and
down the street and up the hill,
Mrs. Cuthbert's
husband snuffed it,
she got nothing from his will.

Mister, mister,
Shirley's sister
won a prize on Blackpool prom,
mam'll smother
our kid brother
when the school inspectors come

Skip and hopping
I'm off shopping,
Tuesday night it's pie for tea,
please to take this
ball and make this
song of bouncing song for me.

TONY CONNOR

The Congo

1 *Their Basic Savagery*

Fat black bucks in a wine-barrel room,
Barrel-house kings, with feet unstable,
Sagged and reeled and pounded on the table,
Pounded on the table,
Beat an empty barrel with the handle of a broom,
Hard as they were able,
Boom, boom, BOOM,
With a silk umbrella and the handle of a broom,
Boomlay, boomlay, boomlay, BOOM.
THEN I had religion, THEN I had a vision.
I could not turn from their revel in derision.
THEN I SAW THE CONGO, CREEPING THROUGH THE BLACK,
CUTTING THROUGH THE FOREST WITH A GOLDEN TRACK.
Then along that riverbank
A thousand miles
Tattooed cannibals danced in files;
Then I heard the boom of the blood-lust song
And a thigh-bone beating on a tin-pan gong.
And 'BLOOD' screamed the whistles and the fifes of the
warriors,
'BLOOD' screamed the skull-faced lean witch-doctors,
'Whirl ye the deadly voo-doo rattle,
Harry the uplands,
Steal all the cattle,
Rattle-rattle, rattle-rattle,
Bing.
Boomlay, boomlay, boomlay, BOOM,'
A roaring, epic, rag-time tune
From the mouth of the Congo
To the mountains of the Moon.
Death is an elephant,
Torch-eyed and horrible,
Foam-flanked and terrible.

BOOM, steal the pygmies,
BOOM, kill the Arabs,
BOOM, kill the white men,
HOO, HOO, HOO.
Listen to the yell of Leopold's ghost
Burning in Hell for his hand-maimed host.
Hear how the demons chuckle and yell
Cutting his hands off, down in Hell.
Listen to the creepy proclamation,
Blown through the lairs of the forest-nation,
Blown past the white ants' hill of clay,
Blown past the marsh where the butterflies play: –
'Be careful what you do,
Or Mumbo-Jumbo, God of the Congo,
And all of the other
Gods of the Congo,
Mumbo-Jumbo will hoo-doo you,
Mumbo-Jumbo will hoo-doo you,
Mumbo-Jumbo will hoo-doo you.'

2 *Their Irrepressible High Spirits*

Wild crap-shooters with a whoop and a call
Danced the juba in their gambling-hall
And laughed fit to kill, and shook the town,
And guyed the policemen and laughed them down
With a boomlay, boomlay, boomlay, BOOM.
THEN I SAW THE CONGO, CREEPING THROUGH THE BLACK,
CUTTING THROUGH THE FOREST WITH A GOLDEN TRACK.
A negro fairyland swung into view,
A minstrel river
Where dreams come true.
The ebony palace soared on high
Through the blossoming trees to the evening sky.
The inlaid porches and casements shone
With gold and ivory and elephant-bone.

And the black crowd laughed till their sides were sore
At the baboon butler in the agate door,
And the well-known tunes of the parrot band
That trilled on the bushes of that magic land.

A troupe of skull-faced witch-men came
Through the agate doorway in suits of flame,
Yea, long-tailed coats with a gold-leaf crust
And hats that were covered with diamond-dust.
And the crowd in the court gave a whoop and a call
And danced the juba from wall to wall.
But the witch-men suddenly stilled the throng
With a stern cold glare, and a stern old song: –
'Mumbo-Jumbo will hoo-doo you.' . . .
Just then from the doorway, as fat as shotes,
Came the cake-walk princes in their long red coats,
Canes with a brilliant lacquer shine,
And tall silk hats that were red as wine.
And they pranced with their butterfly partners there,
Coal-black maidens with pearls in their hair,
Knee-skirts trimmed with the jassamine sweet,
And bells on their ankles and little black feet.
And the couples railed at the chant and the frown
Of the witch-men lean, and laughed them down.
(O rare was the revel, and well worth while
That made those glowering witch-men smile.)

The cake-walk royalty then began
To walk for a cake that was tall as a man
To the tune of 'Boomlay, boomlay, BOOM',
While the witch-men laughed, with a sinister air,
And sang with the scalawags prancing there: –
'Walk with care, walk with care,
Or Mumbo-Jumbo, God of the Congo,
And all of the other
Gods of the Congo,
Mumbo-Jumbo will hoo-doo you.

Beware, beware, walk with care,
Boomlay, boomlay, boomlay, boom,
Boomlay, boomlay, boomlay, boom,
Boomlay, boomlay, boomlay, boom,
Boomlay, boomlay, boomlay,
BOOM.'
Oh rare was the revel, and well worth while
That made those glowering witch-men smile.

3 *The Hope of their Religion*

A good old negro in the slums of the town
Preached at a sister for her velvet gown.
Howled at a brother for his low-down ways,
His prowling, guzzling, sneak-thief days.
Beat on the Bible till he wore it out
Starting the jubilee revival shout.
And some had visions, as they stood on chairs,
And sang of Jacob, and the golden stairs,
And they all repented, a thousand strong
From their stupor and savagery and sin and wrong
And slammed with their hymn books till they shook the room
With 'glory, glory, glory',
And 'Boom, boom, BOOM'.
THEN I SAW THE CONGO, CREEPING THROUGH THE BLACK,
CUTTING THROUGH THE JUNGLE WITH A GOLDEN TRACK.
And the gray sky opened like a new-rent veil
And showed the Apostles with their coats of mail.
In bright white steel they were seated round
And their fire-eyes watched where the Congo wound.
And the twelve Apostles, from their thrones on high
Thrilled all the forest with their heavenly cry: –
'Mumbo-Jumbo will die in the jungle;
Never again will he hoo-doo you,
Never again will he hoo-doo you.'

Then along that river, a thousand miles
The vine-snared trees fell down in files.
Pioneer angels cleared the way
For a Congo paradise, for babes at play,
For sacred capitals, for temples clean.
Gone were the skull-faced witch-men lean.
There, where the wild ghost-gods had wailed
A million boats of the angels sailed
With oars of silver, and prows of blue
And silken pennants that the sun shone through.
'Twas a land transfigured, 'twas a new creation.
Oh, a singing wind swept the negro nation
And on through the backwoods clearing flew: –
'Mumbo-Jumbo is dead in the jungle.
Never again will he hoo-doo you.
Never again will he hoo-doo you.'

Redeemed were the forests, the beasts and the men,
And only the vulture dared again
By the far, lone mountains of the moon
To cry, in the silence, the Congo tune: –
'Mumbo-Jumbo will hoo-doo you,
Mumbo-Jumbo will hoo-doo you.
Mumbo . . . Jumbo . . . will . . . hoo-doo . . . you . . .'

VACHEL LINDSAY

Creative Writing

1 Waves breaking on the sea-shore, the dripping of a tap, horses galloping, a machine doing a repetitive job, your heart beating – all these have very clear, though very different, rhythmic patterns. You could choose one of these, or something else with a regular rhythm, as the subject of a poem. It might help you to look again at W. H. Auden's *Night Mail* on p. 18: notice how he makes the rhythm of his lines suit the subject.

2 Imagine that you are involved in some repetitive exercise – for example, swimming in a race, rowing a boat, playing the drums in a band or pop group, or working a swing higher and higher – and write a poem about what you imagine your feelings would be. How does the rhythm of the action affect the way in which you think and feel? You could try to show this in your poem.

3 Most of you have seen a grandfather clock; some of you may have one in your own home. Imagine that you are a clock ticking his way through the centuries and write a poem telling your life story.

4 The picture of the ballet-dancer on p. 66 may remind some of you of ballet that you have seen on television or at the theatre. A few of you may have been to ballet classes. You may be able to write a poem on this or a similar subject such as ice-skating.

5 Look at Tony Connor's poem *Child's Bouncing Song* on p. 58. It is easy to make up additional verses of your own, although you might find it difficult to get started. One way round this problem is to start, as the poem does, with a person's name. Be sure that your verses have the same pattern as the original: notice the rhythm and which lines rhyme.

Degas

ANIMALS, BIRDS AND INSECTS

Fox

Exploiter of the shadows
He moved among the fences,
A strip of action coiling
Around his farmyard fancies.

With shouting, fields are shaken;
The spinneys give no shelter:
There is delight for riders,
For hounds a tooth in shoulder.

The creature tense with wildness
Knows death is sudden falling
From fury into weary
Surrendering of feeling.

CLIFFORD DYMENT

Carrion

A yellowhammer in her mouth, the cat came mewing
To me. It was such a bird as I had seen
Skim the hedge like a ball of sun
Hurled by a starchild gaming in the wheat.

That was in summer. Now it is autumn,
I burning the leaves of a brave year dead
And gazing at the yellowhammer the cat abandoned,
Shrunken, soaked, but with a bright plume yet.

I stir the body: it is a shell stuffed with maggots.
They uncurl, startled by this threat to life –
And I, with human – so far holy! – love,
Hate maggots and cat, and long for golden wings.

CLIFFORD DYMENT

The Jaguar

The apes yawn and adore their fleas in the sun.
The parrots shriek as if they were on fire, or strut
Like cheap tarts to attract the stroller with the nut.
Fatigued with indolence, tiger and lion

Lie still as the sun. The boa-constrictor's coil
Is a fossil. Cage after cage seems empty, or
Stinks of sleepers from the breathing straw.
It might be painted on a nursery wall.

But who runs like the rest past these arrives
At a cage where the crowd stands, stares, mesmerised,
As a child at a dream, at a jaguar hurrying enraged
Through prison darkness after the drills of his eyes

On a short fierce fuse. Not in boredom –
The eye satisfied to be blind in fire,
By the bang of blood in the brain deaf the ear –
He spins from the bars, but there's no cage to him

More than to the visionary his cell:
His stride is wildernesses of freedom:
The world rolls under the long thrust of his heel.
Over the cage floor the horizons come.

TED HUGHES

The Tyger

Tyger! Tyger! burning bright
In the forests of the night,
What immortal hand or eye
Could frame thy fearful symmetry?

In what distant deeps or skies
Burnt the fire of thine eyes?
On what wings dare he aspire?
What the hand dare seize the fire?

And what shoulder, and what art,
Could twist the sinews of thy heart?
And when thy heart began to beat,
What dread hand? and what dread feet?

What the hammer? what the chain?
In what furnace was thy brain?
What the anvil? what dread grasp
Dare its deadly terrors clasp?

When the stars threw down their spears,
And water'd heaven with their tears,
Did he smile his work to see?
Did he who made the Lamb make thee?

Tyger! Tyger! burning bright
In the forests of the night,
What immortal hand or eye,
Dare frame thy fearful symmetry?

WILLIAM BLAKE

Pigeons

They paddle with staccato feet
In powder-pools of sunlight,
Small blue busybodies
Strutting like fat gentlemen
With hands clasped
Under their swallowtail coats;
And, as they stump about,
Their heads like tiny hammers
Tap at imaginary nails
In non-existent walls.
Elusive ghosts of sunshine
Slither down the green gloss
Of their necks an instant, and are gone.

Summer hangs drugged from sky to earth
In limpid fathoms of silence:
Only warm dark dimples of sound
Slide like slow bubbles
From the contented throats.

Raise a casual hand –
With one quick gust
They fountain into air.

RICHARD KELL

Hedgehog

Twitching the leaves just where the drainpipe clogs
In ivy leaves and mud, a purposeful
Creature at night about its business. Dogs
Fear his stiff seriousness. He chews away

At beetles, worms, slugs, frogs. Can kill a hen
With one snap of his jaws, can taunt a snake
To death on muscled spines. Old countrymen
Tell tales of hedgehogs sucking a cow dry.

But this one, cramped by houses, fences, walls,
Must have slept here all winter in that heap
Of compost, or have inched by intervals
Through tidy gardens to this ivy bed.

And here, dim-eyed, but ears so sensitive
A voice within the house can make him freeze,
He scuffs the edge of danger; yet can live
Happily in our nights and absences.

A country creature, wary, quiet and shrewd,
He takes the milk we give to him, when we're gone.
At night, our slamming voices must seem crude
To one who sits and waits for silences.

ANTHONY THWAITE

The Tom-cat

At midnight in the alley
  A Tom-cat comes to wail,
And he chants the hate of a million years
  As he swings his snaky tail.

Malevolent, bony, brindled,
  Tiger and devil and bard,
His eyes are coals from the middle of Hell
  And his heart is black and hard.

He twists and crouches and capers
  And bares his curved sharp claws,
And he sings to the stars of the jungle nights,
  Ere cities were, or laws.

Beast from a world primeval,
  He and his leaping clan,
When the blotched red moon leers over the roofs
  Give voice to their scorn of man.

He will lie on a rug to-morrow
  And lick his silky fur,
And veil the brute in his yellow eyes
  And play he's tame and purr.

But at midnight in the alley
  He will crouch again and wail,
And beat the time for his demon's song
  With the swing of his demon's tail.

DON MARQUIS

From A Little Bestiary

The Hare

Would rather run up-hill than down-hill;
Would rather look backwards than forwards:
Escapes by going the long way round,
Or by lying still.

Mad? A wild lover,
And a bouncing prize-fighter;
But, a careful mother,
In tussocks of couch-grass
Abandons her leverets.

Wounded, captured, screams
Horribly, like a child;
Is eaten half-putrid, boiled
In its own dark blood;

And is sacred to the Moon,
A type of innocent sacrifice.

The Tortoise

Always to be at home
For the tortoise may be as burdensome
As for the human being,
His continuing exile:

The foxes have hide-outs,
The birds of the air their cradles –
They are free to come and go:
To the tortoise, his dome.

'Stroking, a waste of time,'
(Said Sydney Smith) 'You might as well think,
Caressing St. Paul's, to please
The dean and Chapter,'

But was wrong,
For he is sensitive,
Even to the roof-tops;
Vegetarian, inoffensive, longaeval,
Condemned, through seven generations
Of men, to trundle
The load of his home-keeping.

JOHN HEATH-STUBBS

Two Performing Elephants

He stands with his forefeet on the drum
and the other, the old one, the pallid hoary female
must creep her great bulk beneath the bridge of him.

On her knees, in utmost caution
all agog, and curling up her trunk
she edges through without upsetting him.
Triumph! the ancient, pig-tailed monster!

When her trick is to climb over him
with what shadow-like slow carefulness
she skims him, sensitive
as shadows from the ages gone and perished
in touching him, and planting her round feet.

While the wispy, modern children, half-afraid,
watch silent. The looming of the hoary, far-gone ages
is too much for them.

D. H. LAWRENCE

Death of a Fly

Raising my pen to put a point
On the page, a dot over an i,
An unsteadily veering fly
Collides in a three-point landing, and settles.
Then, as if carving a joint,
It carefully sharpens its legs,
Sitting up the way a dog begs.
I notice a wing shed like a petal.
It has come here to die.
And my dot, streaked now with blood,
Turns the colour of mud.

ALAN ROSS

The Disclosure

From the shrivelling gray
silk of its cocoon
a creature slowly
  is pushing out
to stand clear –
                not a butterfly,
                  petal that floats at will across
                  the summer breeze

                not a furred
                moth of the night
                  crusted with indecipherable
                  gold –

some primal-shaped, plain-winged, day-flying thing.

DENISE LEVERTOV

The Heron

The heron stands in water where the swamp
Has deepened to the blackness of a pool,
Or balances with one leg on a hump
Of marsh grass heaped above a musk-rat hole.

He walks the shallow with an antic grace.
The great feet break the ridges of the sand,
The long eye notes the minnow's hiding place.
His beak is quicker than a human hand.

He jerks a frog across his bony lip,
Then points his heavy bill above the wood.
The wide wings flap but once to lift him up.
A single ripple starts from where he stood.

THEODORE ROETHKE

The Heron

On lonely river-mud a heron alone
Of all things moving – water, reeds, and mist –
Maintains his sculptured attitude of stone.
A dead leaf floats on the sliding river, kissed
By its own reflection in a brief farewell.
Movement without sound; the evening drifts
On autumn tides of colour, light, and smell
Of warm decay; and now the heron lifts
Enormous wings in elegy; a grey
Shadow that seems to bear the light away.

PHOEBE HESKETH

The Rabbit

(*After Prévert*)

We are going to see the rabbit,
We are going to see the rabbit.
Which rabbit, people say?
Which rabbit, ask the children?
Which rabbit?
The only rabbit,
The only rabbit in England,
Sitting behind a barbed-wire fence
Under the floodlights, neon lights,
Sodium lights,
Nibbling grass
On the only patch of grass
In England, in England
(Except the grass by the hoardings
Which doesn't count.)
We are going to see the rabbit
And we must be there on time.

First we shall go by escalator,
Then we shall go by underground,
And then we shall go by motorway
And then by helicopterway,
And the last ten yards we shall have to go
On foot.

And now we are going
All the way to see the rabbit,
We are nearly there,
We are longing to see it,
And so is the crowd
Which is here in thousands

With mounted policemen
And big loudspeakers
And bands and banners,
And everyone has come a long way.
But soon we shall see it
Sitting and nibbling
The blades of grass
On the only patch of grass
In – but something has gone wrong!
Why is everyone so angry,
Why is everyone jostling
And slanging and complaining?

The rabbit has gone,
Yes, the rabbit has gone.
He has actually burrowed down into the earth
And made himself a warren, under the earth,
Despite all these people.
And what shall we do?
What *can* we do?

It is all a pity, you must be disappointed,
Go home and do something else for today,
Go home again, go home for today.
For you cannot hear the rabbit, under the earth,
Remarking rather sadly to himself, by himself,
As he rests in his warren, under the earth:
'It won't be long, they are bound to come,
They are bound to come and find me, even here.'

ALAN BROWNJOHN

Creative Writing

1 John Heath-Stubbs' poems *The Hare* and *The Tortoise* (p. 74) are from what he calls 'A Little Bestiary'. What do you think this phrase means? Perhaps you could write a poem, or even a group of poems, about the animal(s) you would like to see included in a bestiary. You may want to write about imaginary creatures such as dragons, unicorns, the Loch Ness Monster; about prehistoric monsters; about wild animals; or about the more friendly creatures you may have as pets.

2 Which details of the pigeons' movements and appearance seem to you most striking in Richard Kell's poem on p. 70? How does the writer give us such a clear picture? You may be able to write your own poem either about one of the birds you have seen near your home – sparrows, starlings, thrushes, blackbirds, gulls – or about more unusual birds you may have seen in films or books, such as vultures, penguins, owls and ostriches.

Before you begin to write, notice how Richard Kell's pigeons are, in some ways, almost human. You could try to do the same thing in your poem.

3 At some time, all of you will have been in a classroom when a wasp or bee has been flying about.

What is the reaction of the class?

What you do feel when it buzzes around you?

What do you notice about its movement, shape, colour and sound as it knocks angrily against the window-pane?

What are your feelings if you squash it against the glass?

Perhaps you could write a poem describing some or all of these incidents. The picture on p. 77 may help.

4 It is unfortunate that the picture of the peacock on p. 71 is not in colour, but you can still get some idea of his magnificent plumage. Notice how there are several different kinds of feather. Also, look carefully at his head and feet. Can you find phrases or comparisons to describe these details? Does the peacock seem to have a particular character? Perhaps you could write about him.

5 These two photographs are of a human eye and a bee's eye. Try to express the details of the picture in your own words. Are there any comparisons suggested?

You may find it interesting to write a poem based on one of these photographs, or to write a poem on what one can learn about the feelings of, for example, an old man or a baby, a bird or an animal, from looking at their eyes.

BALLADS AND STORIES

The Rime of the Ancient Mariner

PART I

It is an ancient Mariner,
And he stoppeth one of three.
'By thy long grey beard and glittering eye,
Now wherefore stopp'st thou me?

The Bridegroom's doors are opened wide,
And I am next of kin;
The guests are met, the feast is set:
May'st hear the merry din.'

He holds him with his skinny hand,
'There was a ship,' quoth he.
'Hold off! unhand me, grey-beard loon!'
Eftsoons his hand dropt he.

He holds him with his glittering eye –
The Wedding-Guest stood still,
And listens like a three years' child:
The Mariner hath his will.

The Wedding-Guest sat on a stone:
He cannot choose but hear;
And thus spake on that ancient man,
The bright-eyed Mariner.

'The ship was cheered, the harbour cleared,
Merrily did we drop
Below the kirk, below the hill,
Below the lighthouse top.

The Sun came up upon the left,
Out of the sea came he!
And he shone bright, and on the right
Went down into the sea.

Higher and higher every day,
Till over the mast at noon – '
The Wedding-Guest here beat his breast,
For he heard the loud bassoon.

The bride hath paced into the hall,
Red as a rose is she;
Nodding their heads before her goes
The merry minstrelsy.

The Wedding-Guest he beat his breast,
Yet he cannot choose but hear;
And thus spake on that ancient man,
The bright-eyed Mariner.

'And now the Storm-blast came, and he
Was tyrannous and strong:
He struck with his o'ertaking wings,
And chased us south along.

With sloping masts and dipping prow,
As who pursued with yell and blow
Still treads the shadow of his foe,
And forward bends his head,
The ship drove fast, loud roared the blast,
And southward aye we fled.

And now there came both mist and snow,
And it grew wondrous cold:
And ice, mast-high, came floating by,
As green as emerald.

And through the drifts the snowy clifts
Did send a dismal sheen:
Nor shapes of men nor beasts we ken –
The ice was all between.

The ice was here, the ice was there,
The ice was all around:
It cracked and growled, and roared and howled,
Like noises in a swound!

At length did cross an Albatross,
Thorough the fog it came;
As if it had been a Christian soul,
We hailed it in God's name.

It ate the food it ne'er had eat,
And round and round it flew.
The ice did split with a thunder-fit;
The helmsman steered us through!

And a good south wind sprung up behind;
The Albatross did follow,
And every day, for food or play,
Came to the mariners' hollo!

In mist or cloud, on mast or shroud,
It perched for vespers nine;
Whiles all the night, through fog-smoke white,
Glimmered the white moon-shine.'

'God save thee, ancient Mariner!
From the fiends, that plague thee thus! –
Why look'st thou so?' – 'With my cross-bow
I shot the Albatross.

PART II

The Sun now rose upon the right:
Out of the sea came he,
Still hid in mist, and on the left
Went down into the sea.

And the good south wind still blew behind,
But no sweet bird did follow,
Nor any day for food or play
Come to the mariners' hollo!

And I had done a hellish thing,
And it would work 'em woe:
For all averred, I had killed the bird
That made the breeze to blow.
Ah wretch! said they, the bird to slay,
That made the breeze to blow!

Nor dim nor red, like God's own head,
The glorious Sun uprist:
Then all averred, I had killed the bird
That brought the fog and mist.
'Twas right, said they, such birds to slay,
That bring the fog and mist.

The fair breeze blew, the white foam flew,
The furrow followed free;
We were the first that ever burst
Into that silent sea.

Down dropt the breeze, the sails dropt down,
'Twas sad as sad could be;
And we did speak only to break
The silence of the sea!

All in a hot and copper sky,
The bloody Sun, at noon,
Right up above the mast did stand,
No bigger than the Moon.

Day after day, day after day,
We stuck, nor breath nor motion;
As idle as a painted ship
Upon a painted ocean.

Water, water, everywhere,
And all the boards did shrink;
Water, water, everywhere
Nor any drop to drink.

The very deep did rot: O Christ!
That ever this should be!
Yea, slimy things did crawl with legs
Upon the slimy sea.

About, about, in reel and rout
The death-fires danced at night;
The water, like a witch's oils,
Burnt, green and blue and white.

And some in dreams assured were
Of the Spirit that plagued us so;
Nine fathom deep he had followed us
From the land of mist and snow.

And every tongue, through utter drought,
Was withered at the root;
We could not speak, no more than if
We had been choked with soot.

Ah! well a-day! what evil looks
Had I from old and young!
Instead of the cross, the Albatross
About my neck was hung.

PART III

There passed a weary time. Each throat
Was parched, and glazed each eye.
A weary time! a weary time!
How glazed each weary eye,
When looking westward, I beheld
A something in the sky.

At first it seemed a little speck,
And then it seemed a mist;
It moved and moved, and took at last
A certain shape, I wist.

A speck, a mist, a shape, I wist!
And still it neared and neared:
As if it dodged a water-sprite,
It plunged and tacked and veered.

With throats unslaked, with black lips baked,
We could nor laugh nor wail;
Through utter drought all dumb we stood!
I bit my arm, I sucked the blood,
And cried, A sail! a sail!

With throats unslaked, with black lips baked,
Agape they heard me call:
Gramercy! they for joy did grin,
And all at once their breath drew in,
As they were drinking all.

See! see! (I cried) she tacks no more!
Hither to work us weal;
Without a breeze, without a tide,
She steadies with upright keel!

The western wave was all a-flame.
The day was well nigh done!
Almost upon the western wave
Rested the broad bright Sun;
When that strange shape drove suddenly
Betwixt us and the Sun.

And straight the Sun was flecked with bars,
(Heaven's Mother send us grace!)
As if through a dungeon-grate he peered
With broad and burning face.

Alas! (thought I, and my heart beat loud)
How fast she nears and nears!
Are those her sails that glance in the Sun,
Like restless gossameres?

Are those her ribs through which the Sun
Did peer, as through a grate?
And is that Woman all her crew?
Is that a Death? and are there two?
Is Death that woman's mate?

Her lips were red, her looks were free,
Her locks were yellow as gold:
Her skin was as white as leprosy,
The Nightmare Life-in-Death was she,
Who thicks man's blood with cold.

The naked hulk alongside came,
And the twain were casting dice:
"The game is done! I've won! I've won,"
Quoth she, and whistles thrice.

The Sun's rim dips; the stars rush out:
At one stride comes the dark;
With far-heard whisper, o'er the sea,
Off shot the spectre-bark.

We listened and looked sideways up!
Fear at my heart, as at a cup,
My life-blood seemed to sip!
The stars were dim, and thick the night,
The steersman's face by his lamp gleamed white;
From the sails the dew did drip –
Till clomb above the eastern bar
The horned Moon, with one bright star
Within the nether tip.

One after one, by the star-dogged Moon,
Too quick for groan or sigh,
Each turned his face with a ghastly pang,
And cursed me with his eye.

Four times fifty living men,
(And I heard nor sigh nor groan)
With heavy thump, a lifeless lump,
They dropped down one by one.

The souls did from their bodies fly, –
They fled to bliss or woe!
And every soul, it passed me by,
Like the whizz of my cross-bow!'

PART IV

'I fear thee, ancient Mariner!
I fear thy skinny hand!
And thou art long, and lank, and brown,
As is the ribbed sea-sand.

I fear thee and thy glittering eye,
And thy skinny hand, so brown.' –
'Fear not, fear not, thou Wedding-Guest!
This body dropt not down.

Alone, alone, all, all alone,
Alone on a wide wide sea!
And never a saint took pity on
My soul in agony.

The many men, so beautiful!
And they all dead did lie:
And a thousand thousand slimy things
Lived on; and so did I.

I looked upon the rotting sea,
And drew my eyes away;
I looked upon the rotting deck,
And there the dead men lay.

I looked to heaven, and tried to pray;
But or ever a prayer had gusht,
A wicked whisper came, and made
My heart as dry as dust.

I closed my lids, and kept them close,
And the balls like pulses beat;
For the sky and the sea, and the sea and the sky
Lay like a load on my weary eye,
And the dead were at my feet.

The cold sweat melted from their limbs,
Nor rot nor reek did they:
The look with which they looked on me
Had never passed away.

An orphan's curse would drag to hell
A spirit from on high;
But oh! more horrible than that
Is the curse in a dead man's eye!
Seven days, seven nights, I saw that curse,
And yet I could not die.

The moving Moon went up the sky,
And no where did abide:
Softly she was going up,
And a star or two beside –

Her beams bemocked the sultry main,
Like April hoar-frost spread;
But where the ship's huge shadow lay,
The charmed water burnt alway
A still and awful red.

Beyond the shadow of the ship,
I watched the water-snakes:
They moved in tracks of shining white,
And when they reared, the elfish light
Fell off in hoary flakes.

Within the shadow of the ship
I watched their rich attire:
Blue, glossy green, and velvet black,
They coiled and swam; and every track
Was a flash of golden fire.

O happy living things! no tongue
Their beauty might declare:
A spring of love gushed from my heart,
And I blessed them unaware:
Sure my kind saint took pity on me,
And I blessed them unaware.

The self-same moment I could pray;
And from my neck so free
The Albatross fell off, and sank
Like lead into the sea.

Part V

Oh sleep! it is a gentle thing,
Beloved from pole to pole!
To Mary Queen the praise be given!
She sent the gentle sleep from Heaven,
That slid into my soul.

The silly buckets on the deck,
That had so long remained,
I dreamt that they were filled with dew;
And when I awoke, it rained.

My lips were wet, my throat was cold,
My garments all were dank;
Sure I had drunken in my dreams,
And still my body drank.

I moved, and could not feel my limbs:
I was so light – almost
I thought that I had died in sleep,
And was a blessed ghost.

And soon I heard a roaring wind:
It did not come anear;
But with its sound it shook the sails,
That were so thin and sere.

The upper air burst into life!
And a hundred fire-flags sheen,
To and fro they were hurried about!
And to and fro, and in and out,
The wan stars danced between.

And the coming wind did roar more loud,
And the sails did sigh like sedge;
And the rain poured down from one black cloud;
The Moon was at its edge.

The thick black cloud was cleft, and still
The Moon was at its side:
Like waters shot from some high crag,
The lightning fell with never a jag,
A river steep and wide.

The loud wind never reached the ship,
Yet now the ship moved on!
Beneath the lightning and the Moon
The dead men gave a groan.

They groaned, they stirred, they all uprose,
Nor spake, nor moved their eyes:
It had been strange, even in a dream,
To have seen those dead men rise.

The helmsman steered, the ship moved on:
Yet never a breeze up-blew;
The mariners all 'gan work the ropes,
Where they were wont to do;
They raised their limbs like lifeless tools –
We were a ghastly crew.

The body of my brother's son
Stood by me, knee to knee:
The body and I pulled at one rope,
But he said nought to me.'

'I fear thee, ancient Mariner!'
'Be calm, thou Wedding-Guest!
'Twas not those souls that fled in pain,
Which to their corses came again,
But a troop of spirits blest:

For when it dawned – they dropped their arms,
And clustered round the mast;
Sweet sounds rose slowly through their mouths,
And from their bodies passed.

Around, around, flew each sweet sound,
Then darted to the Sun;
Slowly the sounds came back again,
Now mixed, now one by one.

Sometimes a-drooping from the sky
I heard the sky-lark sing;
Sometimes all little birds that are,
How they seemed to fill the sea and air
With their sweet jargoning!

And now 'twas like all instruments,
Now like a lonely flute;
And now it is an angel's song,
That makes the heavens be mute.

It ceased; yet still the sails made on
A pleasant noise till noon,
A noise like of a hidden brook
In the leafy month of June,
That to the sleeping woods all night
Singeth a quiet tune.

Till noon we quietly sailed on,
Yet never a breeze did breathe:
Slowly and smoothly went the ship,
Moved onward from beneath.

Under the keel nine fathom deep,
From the land of mist and snow,
The spirit slid: and it was he
That made the ship to go.
The sails at noon left off their tune,
And the ship stood still also.

The Sun, right up above the mast,
Had fixed her to the ocean:
But in a minute she 'gan stir,
With a short uneasy motion –
Backwards and forwards half her length
With a short uneasy motion.

Then like a pawing horse let go,
She made a sudden bound:
It flung the blood into my head,
And I fell down in a swound.

How long in that same fit I lay,
I have not to declare;
But ere my living life returned,
I heard and in my soul discerned
Two voices in the air.

"Is it he?" quoth one, "Is this the man?
By him who died on cross,
With his cruel bow he laid full low
The harmless Albatross.

The spirit who bideth by himself
In the land of mist and snow,
He loved the bird that loved the man
Who shot him with his bow."

The other was a softer voice,
As soft as honey-dew:
Quoth he, "The man hath penance done,
And penance more will do."

Part VI

First Voice
"But tell me, tell me! speak again,
Thy soft response renewing –
What makes that ship drive on so fast?
What is the ocean doing?"

Second Voice
"Still as a slave before his lord,
The ocean hath no blast;
His great bright eye most silently
Up to the Moon is cast –

If he may know which way to go;
For she guides him smooth or grim.
See, brother, see! how graciously
She looketh down on him."

First Voice
"But why drives on that ship so fast,
Without or wave or wind?"

Second Voice
"The air is cut away before,
And closes from behind.

Fly, brother, fly! more high, more high!
Or we shall be belated:
For slow and slow that ship will go,
When the Mariner's trance is abated."

I woke and we were sailing on
As in a gentle weather:
'Twas night, calm night, the moon was high;
The dead men stood together.

All stood together on the deck,
For a charnel-dungeon fitter:
All fixed on me their stony eyes,
That in the Moon did glitter.

The pang, the curse, with which they died,
Had never passed away:
I could not draw my eyes from theirs,
Nor turn them up to pray.

And now this spell was snapt: once more
I viewed the ocean green,
And looked far forth, yet little saw
Of what had else been seen –

Like one, that on a lonesome road
Doth walk in fear and dread,
And having once turned round walks on,
And turns no more his head;
Because he knows, a frightful fiend
Doth close behind him tread.

But soon there breathed a wind on me,
Nor sound nor motion made:
Its path was not upon the sea,
In ripple or in shade.

It raised my hair, it fanned my cheek
Like a meadow-gale of spring –
It mingled strangely with my fears,
Yet it felt like a welcoming.

Swiftly, swiftly flew the ship,
Yet she sailed softly too:
Sweetly, sweetly blew the breeze –
On me alone it blew.

Oh! dream of joy! is this indeed
The light-house top I see?
Is this the hill? is this the kirk?
Is this mine own countree?

We drifted o'er the harbour-bar,
And I with sobs did pray –
O let me be awake, my God!
Or let me sleep alway.

The harbour-bay was clear as glass,
So smoothly it was strewn!
And on the bay the moonlight lay,
And the shadow of the Moon.

The rock shone bright, the kirk no less,
That stands above the rock:
The moonlight steeped in silentness
The steady weathercock.

And the bay was white with silent light,
Till rising from the same,
Full many shapes, that shadows were,
In crimson colours came.

A little distance from the prow
Those crimson shadows were:
I turned my eyes upon the deck –
Oh, Christ! what saw I there!

Each corse lay flat, lifeless and flat,
And, by the holy rood!
A man all light, a seraph-man,
On every corse there stood,

This seraph-band, each waved his hand:
It was a heavenly sight!
They stood as signals to the land,
Each one a lovely light;

This seraph-band, each waved his hand,
No voice did they impart –
No voice; but oh! the silence sank
Like music on my heart.

But soon I heard the dash of oars.
I heard the Pilot's cheer;
My head was turned perforce away
And I saw a boat appear.

The Pilot and the Pilot's boy,
I heard them coming fast:
Dear Lord in Heaven! it was a joy
The dead men could not blast.

I saw a third – I heard his voice:
It is the Hermit good!
He singeth loud his godly hymns
That he makes in the wood.
He'll shrieve my soul, he'll wash away
The Albatross's blood.

Part VII

This Hermit good lives in that wood
Which slopes down to the sea.
How loudly his sweet voice he rears!
He loves to talk with marineres
That come from a far countree.

He kneels at morn, and noon, and eve –
He hath a cushion plump:
It is the moss that wholly hides
The rotted old oak-stump.

The skiff-boat neared: I heard them talk,
"Why, this is strange, I trow!
Where are those lights so many and fair,
That signal made but now?"

"Strange, by my faith!" the Hermit said –
"And they answered not our cheer!
The planks looked warped! and see those sails,
How thin they are and sere!
I never saw aught like to them,
Unless perchance it were

Brown skeletons of leaves that lag
My forest-brook along;
When the ivy-tod is heavy with snow,
And the owlet whoops to the wolf below,
That eats the she-wolf's young."

"Dear Lord! it hath a fiendish look" –
(The Pilot made reply)
"I am a-feared" – "Push on, push on!"
Said the Hermit cheerily.

The boat came closer to the ship,
But I nor spake nor stirred;
The boat came close beneath the ship,
And straight a sound was heard.

Under the water it rumbled on,
Still louder and more dread:
It reached the ship, it split the bay;
The ship went down like lead.

Stunned by that loud and dreadful sound,
Which sky and ocean smote,
Like one that hath been seven days drowned
My body lay afloat;
But swift as dreams, myself I found
Within the Pilot's boat.

Upon the whirl, where sank the ship,
The boat spun round and round;
And all was still, save that the hill
Was telling of the sound.

I moved my lips – the Pilot shrieked
And fell down in a fit;
The holy Hermit raised his eyes,
And prayed where he did sit.

I took the oars: the Pilot's boy,
Who now doth crazy go,
Laughed loud and long, and all the while
His eyes went to and fro.
"Ha! ha!" quoth he, "full plain I see,
The Devil knows how to row."

And now, all in my own countree,
I stood on the firm land!
The Hermit stepped forth from the boat,
And scarcely he could stand.

"O shrieve me, shrieve me, holy man!"
The Hermit crossed his brow.
"Say quick," quoth he, "I bid thee say –
What manner of man art thou?"

Forthwith this frame of mine was wrenched
With a woful agony,
Which forced me to begin my tale;
And then it left me free.

Since then, at an uncertain hour,
That agony returns:
And till my ghastly tale is told,
This heart within me burns.

I pass, like night, from land to land;
I have strange power of speech;
That moment that his face I see,
I know the man that must hear me:
To him my tale I teach.

What loud uproar bursts from that door!
The wedding-guests are there:
But in the garden-bower the bride
And bride-maids singing are:
And hark the little vesper bell,
Which biddeth me to prayer!

O Wedding-Guest! this soul hath been
Alone on a wide wide sea:
So lonely 'twas, that God himself
Scarce seemed there to be.

O sweeter than the marriage-feast,
'Tis sweeter far to me,
To walk together to the kirk
With a goodly company! –

To walk together to the kirk,
And all together pray,
While each to his great Father bends,
Old men, and babes, and loving friends
And youths and maidens gay!

Farewell, farewell! but this I tell
To thee, thou Wedding-Guest!
He prayeth well, who loveth well
Both man and bird and beast.

He prayeth best, who loveth best
All things both great and small;
For the dear God who loveth us,
He made and loveth all.'

The Mariner, whose eye is bright,
Whose beard with age is hoar,
Is gone: and now the Wedding Guest
Turned from the bridegroom's door.

He went like one that hath been stunned,
And is of sense forlorn:
A sadder and a wiser man,
He rose the morrow morn.

S. T. COLERIDGE

I Started Early

I started early, took my dog,
  And visited the sea.
The mermaids in the basement
  Came out to look at me

And frigates in the upper floor
  Extended hempen hands,
Presuming me to be a mouse
  Aground upon the sands,

But no man moved me till the tide
  Went past my simple shoe
And past my apron and my belt
  And past my bodice too,

And made as he would eat me up
  As wholly as a dew
Upon a dandelion's sleeve;
  And then I started too

And he, he followed close behind;
  I felt his silver heel
Upon my ankle, then my shoes
  Would overflow with pearl,

Until we met the solid town.
  No one he seemed to know
And bowing with a mighty look
  At me, the sea withdrew.

EMILY DICKINSON

The Sea Serpent Chantey

There's a snake on the western wave
And his crest is red.
He is long as a city street,
And he eats the dead.
There's a hole in the bottom of the sea
Where the snake goes down.
And he waits in the bottom of the sea
For the men that drown.

  Chorus:–
  This is the voice of the sand
  (The sailors understand)
  'There is far more sea than sand,
  There is far more sea than land.
  Yo . . . ho, yo . . . ho.'

He waits by the door of his cave
While the ages moan.
He cracks the ribs of the ships
With his teeth of stone.
In his gizzard deep and long
Much treasure lies.
Oh, the pearls and the Spanish gold. . . .
And the idols' eyes. . . .
Oh, the totem poles . . . the skulls . . .
The altars cold . . .
The wedding rings, the dice . . .
The buoy bells old.

Chorus: –
This is the voice of the sand
(The sailors understand)
'There is far more sea than sand,
There is far more sea than land.
Yo . . . ho, yo . . . ho.'

Dive, meremaids, with sharp swords
And cut him through,
And bring us the idols' eyes
And the red gold too.
Lower the grappling hooks
Good pirate men
And drag him up by the tongue
From his deep wet den.
We will sail to the end of the world,
We will nail his hide
To the mainmast of the moon
In the evening tide.
Chorus: –
This is the voice of the sand
(The sailors understand)
'There is far more sea than sand,
There is far more sea than land.
Yo . . . ho, yo . . . ho.'

Or will you let him live,
The deep-sea thing,
With the wrecks of all the world
In a black wide ring
By the hole in the bottom of the sea
Where the snake goes down,
Where he waits in the bottom of the sea
For the men that drown?

Chorus: –
This is the voice of the sand
(The sailors understand)
'There is far more sea than sand,
There is far more sea than land.
Yo . . . ho, yo . . . ho.'

VACHEL LINDSAY

Finnegan's Wake

Tim Finnegan liv'd in Walkin Street,
A gentleman Irish mighty odd.
He had a tongue both rich and sweet,
An' to rise in the world he carried a hod,
Now Tim had a sort of a tipplin' way
With the love of the liquor he was born,
An' to help him on with his work each day,
He'd a drop of the craythur ev'ry morn.
Whack fol the dah, dance to your partner
Welt the flure, yer trotters shake,
Wasn't it the truth I told you,
Lots of fun at Finnegan's Wake.

One morning Tim was rather full,
His head felt heavy which make him shake,
He fell from the ladder and broke his skull,
So they carried him home his corpse to wake,
They rolled him up in a nice clean sheet,
And laid him out upon the bed,
With a gallon of whiskey at his feet,
And a barrel of porter at his head.

His friends assembled at the wake,
And Mrs. Finnegan called for lunch,
First they brought in tay and cake,
Then pipes, tobacco, and whiskey punch.
Miss Biddy O'Brien began to cry,
'Such a neat clean corpse, did you ever see,
Arrah, Tim avourneen, why did you die?'
'Ah, hould your gab,' said Paddy McGee.

Then Biddy O'Connor took up the job,
'Biddy,' says she, 'you're wrong, I'm sure,'
But Biddy gave her a belt in the gob,
And left her sprawling on the floor;
Oh, then the war did soon enrage;
'Twas woman to woman and man to man,
Shillelagh law did all engage,
And a row and a ruction soon began.

Then Mickey Maloney raised his head,
When a noggin of whiskey flew at him,
It missed and falling on the bed,
The liquor scattered over Tim;
Bedad he revives, see how he rises,
And Timothy rising from the bed,
Says, 'Whirl your liquor round like blazes,
Thanam o'n dhoul, do ye think I'm dead?'
Whack fol the dah, dance to your partner
Welt the flure, yer trotters shake,
Wasn't it the truth I told you,
Lots of fun at Finnegan's Wake.

ANON

Casey Jones

Come all you rounders if you want to hear
The story of a brave engineer;
Casey Jones was the hogger's name,
On a big eight-wheeler, boys, he won his fame.
Caller called Casey at half-past four,
He kissed his wife at the station door,
Mounted to the cabin with orders in his hand,
And took his farewell trip to the promised land.

Casey Jones, he mounted to the cabin,
Casey Jones, with his orders in his hand!
Casey Jones, he mounted to the cabin,
Took his farewell trip into the promised land.

Put in your water and shovel in your coal,
Put your head out the window, watch the drivers roll,
I'll run her till she leaves the rail,
'Cause we're eight hours late with the Western Mail!
He looked at his watch and his watch was slow,
Looked at the water and the water was low,
Turned to his fireboy and said,
'We'll get to 'Frisco, but we'll all be dead!'
(*Refrain*)

Casey pulled up Reno Hill,
Tooted for the crossing with an awful shrill,
Snakes all knew by the engine's moans
That the hogger at the throttle was Casey Jones.
He pulled up short two miles from the place,
Number Four stared him right in the face,
Turned to his fireboy, said 'You'd better jump,
'Cause there's two locomotives that's going to bump!'
(*Refrain*)

Casey said, just before he died,
'There's two more roads I'd like to ride.'
Fireboy said, 'What can they be?'
'The Rio Grande and the old S.P.'
Mrs. Jones sat on her bed a-sighing,
Got a pink that Casey was dying,
Said, 'Go to bed, children; hush your crying,
'Cause you've got another papa on the Salt Lake Line.'

Casey Jones! Got another papa!
Casey Jones, on the Salt Lake Line!
Casey Jones! Got another papa!
Got another papa on the Salt Lake Line!

ANON

HUMOUR

Tim Turpin

Tim Turpin he was gravel blind,
And ne'er had seen the skies;
For Nature when his head was made,
Forgot to dot his eyes.

So, like a Christmas pedagogue,
Poor Tim was forced to do –
Look out for pupils; for he had
A vacancy for two.

There's some have specs to help their sight
Of objects dim and small:
But Tim had *specks* within his eyes,
And could not see at all.

Now Tim he wooed a servant maid,
And took her to his arms;
For he, like Pyramus, had cast
A wall-eye on her charms.

By day she led him up and down,
Where'er he wished to jog,
A happy wife, altho' she led
The life of any dog.

But just when Tim had lived a month
In honey with his wife,
A surgeon ope'd his Milton eyes,
Like oysters, with a knife.

But when his eyes were opened thus,
He wished them dark again:
For when he looked upon his wife,
He saw her very plain.

Her face was bad, her figure worse,
He couldn't bear to eat:
For she was anything but like
A grace before his meat.

Now Tim he was a feeling man;
For when his sight was thick
It made him feel for everything –
But that was with a stick.

So, with a cudgel in his hand –
It was not light or slim –
He knocked at his wife's head until
It opened unto him.

And when the corpse was stiff and cold,
He took his slaughtered spouse,
And laid her in a heap with all
The ashes of her house.

But like a wicked murderer,
He lived in constant fear
From day to day, and so he cut
His throat from ear to ear.

The neighbours fetched a doctor in;
Said he, 'This wound I dread
Can hardly be sewed up – his life
Is hanging on a thread.'

But when another week was gone,
He gave him stronger hope –
Instead of hanging on a thread,
Of hanging on a rope.

Ah! when he hid his bloody work
In ashes round about,
How little he supposed the truth
Would soon be sifted out.

But when the parish dustman came,
His rubbish to withdraw,
He found more dust within the heap
Than he contracted for!

A dozen men to try the fact
Were sworn that very day;
But though they all were jurors, yet
No conjurors were they.

Said Tim unto those jurymen,
You need not waste your breath,
For I confess myself at once
The author of her death.

And, oh! when I reflect upon
The blood that I have spilt,
Just like a button is my soul,
Inscribed with double *guilt*!

Then turning round his head again,
He saw before his eyes,
A great judge, and a little judge,
The judges of a-size!

The great judge took his judgment cap,
And put it on his head,
And sentenced Tim by law to hang
Till he was three times dead.

So he was tried, and he was hung
(Fit punishment for such)
On Horsham-drop, and none can say
It was a drop too much.

THOMAS HOOD

Domestic Asides; or, Truth in Parentheses

'I really take it very kind,
This visit, Mrs. Skinner!
I have not seen you such an age –
(The wretch has come to dinner!)

'Your daughters, too, what loves of girls –
What heads for painters' easels!
Come here and kiss the infant, dears –
(And give it perhaps the measles!)

'Your charming boys I see are home
From Reverend Mr. Russell's;
'Twas very kind to bring them both –
(What boots for my new Brussels!)

'What! little Clara left at home?
Well now I call that shabby:
I should have loved to kiss her so –
(A flabby, dabby, babby!)

'And Mr. S., I hope he's well,
Ah! though he lives so handy,
He never now drops in to sup –
(The better for our brandy!)

'Come, take a seat – I long to hear
About Matilda's marriage;
You're come of course to spend the day!
(Thank Heaven, I hear the carriage!)

'What! must you go? next time I hope
You'll give me longer measure;
Nay – I shall see you down the stairs –
(With most uncommon pleasure!)

'Good-bye! good-bye! remember all,
Next time you'll take your dinners!
(Now, David, mind I'm not at home
In future to the Skinners!)'

THOMAS HOOD

The Two Old Bachelors

Two old Bachelors were living in one house;
One caught a Muffin, the other caught a Mouse.
Said he who caught the Muffin to him who caught the
  Mouse, –
'This happens just in time! For we've nothing in the house,
'Save a tiny slice of lemon and a teaspoonful of honey,
'And what to do for dinner – since we haven't any money?
'And what can we expect if we haven't any dinner,
'But to lose our teeth and eyelashes and keep on growing
  thinner?'

Said he who caught the Mouse to him who caught the
  Muffin, –
'We might cook this little Mouse, if we only had some
  Stuffin'!
'If we had but Sage and Onion we could do extremely well,
'But how to get that Stuffin' it is difficult to tell!'

Those two old Bachelors ran quickly to the town
And asked for Sage and Onion as they wandered up and
  down;
They borrowed two large Onions, but no Sage was to be
  found
In the Shops, or in the Market, or in all the Gardens round.

But some one said, – 'A hill there is, a little to the north,
'And to its purpledicular top a narrow way leads forth; –
'And there among the rugged rocks abides an ancient Sage, –
'An earnest Man, who reads all day a most perplexing page.

'Climb up, and seize him by the toes! – all studious as he
  sits, –
'And pull him down, – and chop him into endless little bits!
'Then mix him with your Onion (cut up likewise into Scraps), –
'When your Stuffin' will be ready – and very good: perhaps.'

Those two old Bachelors without loss of time
The nearly purpledicular crags at once began to climb;
And at the top, among the rocks, all seated in a nook,
They saw that Sage, a-reading of a most enormous book.
'You earnest Sage!' aloud they cried, 'your book you've read enough in! –
'We wish to chop you into bits to mix you into Stuffin'!'

But that old Sage looked calmly up, and with his awful book,
At those two Bachelors' bald heads a certain aim he took; –
And over Crag and precipice they rolled promiscuous down, –
At once they rolled, and never stopped in lane or field or town, –
And when they reached their house, they found (beside their want of Stuffin'),
The Mouse had fled; – and, previously, had eaten up the Muffin.

They left their home in silence by the once convivial door,
And from that hour those Bachelors were never heard of more.

EDWARD LEAR

Forth From His Den

Forth from his den to steal he stole.
His bag of chink he chunk,
And many a wicked smile he smole,
And many a wink he wunk.

ANON

The Hunter

The hunter crouches in his blind
'Neath camouflage of every kind,
And conjures up a quacking noise
To lend allure to his decoys.
This grown-up man, with pluck and luck,
Is hoping to outwit a duck.

OGDEN NASH

The Eel

I don't mind eels
Except as meals.
And the way they feels.

OGDEN NASH

The Termite

Some primal termite knocked on wood
And tasted it, and found it good,
And that is why your cousin May
Fell through the parlor floor today.

OGDEN NASH

The Firefly

The firefly's flame
Is something for which science has no name.
I can think of nothing eerier
Than flying around with an unidentified glow on a person's
posteerier.

OGDEN NASH

Four Limericks

There was a young man of Montrose
Who had pockets in none of his clothes.
  When asked by his lass
  Where he carried his brass
He said 'Darling, I pay through the nose.'

ARNOLD BENNETT

There was an old fellow of Tring
Who, when somebody asked him to sing,
  Replied, 'Ain't it odd?
  I can never tell *God*
Save the Weasel from *Pop goes the King*.'

ANON

There was an old man from Darjeeling,
Who boarded a bus bound for Ealing.
  He saw on the door:
  'Please don't spit on the floor',
So he stood up and spat on the ceiling.

ANON

There was an old man from Dunoon,
Who always ate soup with a fork,
  For he said, 'As I eat
  Neither fish, fowl nor flesh,
I should finish my dinner too quick.'

ANON

If we parody a piece of writing we poke fun at it by imitating its style. You will quickly see what we mean when you read John Betjeman's poem below which parodies a well-known hymn.

Harvest Hymn

We spray the fields and scatter
  The poison on the ground
So that no wicked wild flowers
  Upon our farm be found.
We like whatever helps us
  To line our purse with pence
The twenty-four-hour broiler-house
  And neat electric fence.

All concrete sheds around us
  And Jaguars in the yard,
The telly lounge and deep-freeze
  Are ours from working hard.

We fire the fields for harvest,
  The hedges swell the flame,
The oak trees and the cottages
  From which our fathers came.
We give no compensation,
  The earth is ours today,
And if we lose on arable,
  Then bungalows will pay.

All concrete sheds . . . etc.

JOHN BETJEMAN

From Hiawatha

Swift of foot was Hiawatha;
He could shoot an arrow from him,
And run forward with such fleetness
That the arrow fell behind him!
Strong of arm was Hiawatha;
He could shoot ten arrows upward,
Shoot them with such strength and swiftness,
That the tenth had left the bowstring
Ere the first to earth had fallen!
He had mittens, Minjekahwun,
Magic mittens made of deer-skin.
When upon his hands he wore them,
He could smite the rocks asunder,
He could grind them into powder.
He had moccasins enchanted,
Magic moccasins of deer-skin;
When he bound them round his ankles,
When upon his feet he tied them,
At each stride a mile he measured!

H. W. LONGFELLOW

The Modern Hiawatha

When he killed the Mudjokivis,
Of the skin he made him mittens,
Made them with the fur side inside,
Made them with the skin side outside,
He, to get the warm side inside,
Put the inside skin side outside.
He, to get the cold side outside,
Put the warm side fur side inside,
That's why he put the fur side inside,
Why he put the skin side outside,
Why he turned them inside outside.

ANON

Creative Writing

1 Take any poem in this anthology and write a parody of it. It is probably best to choose one with a well-defined rhythm: the poems in the section beginning on p. 53 should help you here.
2 Some of you will be used to writing limericks already. For those of you who are not, remember to imitate the regular rhythm and rhymes of the poems on p. 120. Write one or two limericks of your own on any subjects you like.
3 Ogden Nash's poems on p. 119 describe three creatures in a humorous way. Are there any animals that you find particularly amusing? Perhaps you could write a short poem about one of them in a similar style.
4 Thomas Hood's poem *Domestic Asides* on p. 115 is amusing because it tells us not only what the narrator says but also what she really thinks. There must be many people who are put in a position where they cannot speak their mind but have to be polite: for example, a schoolboy or girl being reprimanded by a teacher, a shop-assistant dealing with a particularly difficult customer who keeps changing her mind, or a person trying to be enthusiastic about a present that he dislikes. Try to write your own poem about one of these or a similar situation.

WEATHER

Rain

Rain
When it falls on land
Is a strange element, owned
By gutters and ponds and pools;
Welcome, yet other,
To buds whose wheels it greases,
Mineral, yet not quite brother,
To dust and stone and sand.
On land we keep account of rain
By watching clouds and hearing the drip in the eaves
And knowing the smell of it among the leaves.

But rain
When it falls on sea
Is scarcely seen or heard or smelt
But only felt –
As if a skelter of birds with pittering feet
Were letting on the glass roof of the waves.
The unsalt water falling through the passive air
Has not identity there
Where each drop tastes of the full Atlantic brine.
Back again in the sea
Rain
Is only sea again.

NORMAN NICHOLSON

Early Rain

After the long drought
The sun goes quickly out.
Leaf after leaf in the laden trees
Like cats' ears flick.
Dusty flowers on a dry stick
Stagger beneath the blows
Of the downpour breeze.
Each tree is a sounding drum,
And every rose
Is trampled in the hum
Of the shower's watery bees.

JAMES KIRKUP

Winter-piece

You wake, all windows blind – embattled sprays
grained on the medieval glass.
Gates snap like gunshot
as you handle them. Five-barred fragility
sets flying fifteen rooks who go together
silently ravenous above this winter-piece
that will not feed them. They alight
beyond, scavenging, missing everything
but the bladed atmosphere, the white resistance.
Ruts with iron flanges track
through a hard decay
where you discern once more
oak-leaf by hawthorn, for the frost
rewhets their edges. In a perfect web
blanched along each spoke
and circle of its woven wheel,

the spider hangs, grasp unbroken
and death-masked in cold. Returning
you see the house glint-out behind
its holed and ragged glaze,
frost-fronds all streaming.

CHARLES TOMLINSON

Hard Frost

Frost called to water 'Halt!'
And crusted the moist snow with sparkling salt;
Brooks, their own bridges, stop,
And icicles in long stalactites drop,
And tench in water-holes
Lurk under gluey glass like fish in bowls.

In the hard-rutted lane
At every footstep breaks a brittle pane,
And tinkling trees ice-bound,
Changed into weeping willows, sweep the ground;
Dead boughs take root in ponds
And ferns on windows shoot their ghostly fronds.

But vainly the fierce frost
Interns poor fish, ranks trees in an armed host,
Hangs daggers from house-eaves
And on the windows ferny ambush weaves;
In the long war grown warmer
The sun will strike him dead and strip his armour.

ANDREW YOUNG

Fog

The fog comes
on little cat feet.

It sits looking
over harbour and city
on silent haunches
and then moves on.

CARL SANDBURG

Storm in the Black Forest

Now it is almost night, from the bronzey soft sky
jugfull after jugfull of pure white liquid fire, bright white
tipples over and spills down,
and is gone
and gold-bronze flutters bent through the thick upper air.

And as the electric liquid pours out, sometimes
a still brighter white snake wriggles among it, spilled
and tumbling wriggling down the sky:
and then the heavens cackle with uncouth sounds.

And the rain won't come, the rain refuses to come!

This is the electricity that man is supposed to have mastered,
chained, subjugated to his use!
supposed to!

D. H. LAWRENCE

The Storm

Against the stone breakwater,
Only an ominous lapping,
While the wind whines overhead,
Coming down from the mountain,
Whistling between the arbours, the winding terraces;
A thin whine of wires, a rattling and flapping of leaves,
And the small streetlamp swinging and slamming against the
lamp-pole.
Where have the people gone?
There is one light on the mountain.
Along the sea-wall a steady sloshing of the swell,

The waves not yet high, but even,
Coming closer and closer upon each other;
A fine fume of rain driving in from the sea,
Riddling the sand, like a wide spray of buckshot,
The wind from the sea and the wind from the mountain
  contending,
Flicking the foam from the whitecaps straight upwards into
  the darkness.
A time to go home!
And a child's dirty shift billows upward out of an alley;
A cat runs from the wind as we do,
Between the whitening trees, up Santa Lucia.
Where the heavy door unlocks
And our breath comes more easy.
Then a crack of thunder, and the black rain runs over us, over
The flat-roofed houses, coming down in gusts, beating
The walls, the slatted windows, driving
The last watcher indoors, moving the cardplayers closer
To their cards, their Lachryma Christi.
We creep to our bed and its straw mattress.
We wait, we listen.
The storm lulls off, then redoubles,
Bending the trees halfway down to the ground,
Shaking loose the last wizened oranges in the orchard,
Flattening the limber carnations.
A spider eases himself down from a swaying light bulb,
Running over the coverlet, down under the iron bedstead.
The bulb goes on and off, weakly.
Water roars in the cistern.
We lie closer on the gritty pillow,
Breathing heavily, hoping –
For the great last leap of the wave over the breakwater,
The flat boom on the beach of the towering sea-swell,
The sudden shudder as the jutting sea-cliff collapses
And the hurricane drives the dead straw into the living
  pine-tree.

THEODORE ROETHKE

A Storm

Somebody is throttling that tree
By the way it's threshing about;
I'm glad it's no one I know, or me,
The head thrust back at the throat,

Green hair tumbled and cracking throat.
His thumbs drive into her windpipe,
She cannot cry out,
Only swishing and groaning: death swells ripe,

The light is dimming but the fight goes on.
Chips strike my window. In the morning, there
Stands the tree, still, bushy and calm,
Not as I saw it, twisted heel to ear,

But fluffed up, boughs chafing slightly.
What's become of her attacker?
I'm glad he's not mine or known to me,
Flipped to the ground, heel over ear:

She preens herself, with a soft bough-purr.
Was he swallowed up, lip over ear?
He's gone anyway. The path is thick in her fur.
Am I a friend, may I walk near?

PETER REDGROVE

Snow

Ridged thickly on black bough
  And foaming on twig-fork in swollen lumps
At flirt of bird-wing or wind's sough
  Plump snow tumbled on snow softly with sudden dumps.

Where early steps had made
  A wavering track through the white-blotted road
Breaking its brightness with blue shade,
  Snow creaked beneath my feet with snow heavily shod.

I reached a snow-thatched rick
   Where men sawed bedding off for horse and cow;
There varnished straws were lying thick
   Paving with streaky gold the trodden silver snow.

Such light filled me with awe,
   And nothing marred my paradisal thought,
That robin least of all I saw
   Lying too fast asleep, his song choked in his throat.

ANDREW YOUNG

A Hot Day

Cottonwool clouds loiter.
A lawnmower, very far,
Birrs. Then a bee comes
To a crimson rose and softly,
Deftly and fatly crams
A velvet body in.

A tree, June-lazy, makes
A tent of dim green light.
Sunlight weaves in the leaves,
Honey-light laced with leaf-light,
Green interleaved with gold.
Sunlight gathers its rays
In sheaves, which the wind unweaves
And then reweaves – the wind
That puffs a smell of grass
Through the heat-heavy, trembling
Summer pool of air.

A. S. J. TESSIMOND

Creative Writing

1 Nearly every day you can see many different cloud formations. Perhaps you are already aware of some of the types, from the high, wispy cirrus to the massive, dark storm-clouds, and of their weird, changing shapes. If you look carefully you will find that imaginary pictures of animals, people, objects and places are constantly forming and dissolving. Write a poem about cloud shapes.

2 A. S. J. Tessimond's poem, *A Hot Day*, on p. 134 suggests the drowsiness of hot summer weather. Notice how he selects a few striking details and uses words which, by their sound as well as their meaning, create a gentle and unhurried atmosphere. You may be able to write your own poem, with the same title, which describes the effect of heat on things around you. For example, how does the sun affect flowers, ponds and puddles, your pet dog or cat, people's dress, movements and behaviour?

3 Look at the photograph on p. 132. Freshly fallen snow is often exciting because it makes us see things in a different way. Can you think of comparisons or phrases to describe the snow, the twigs, the effect of sunlight on the snow, the tree in the background? Can you put into words what the photographer has captured on film?

4 Have you noticed what happens when snow begins to thaw? Here are some ideas to set you thinking, but first be clear in your own mind about the place which you are going to write about.

Jot down phrases and comparisons to describe what you see and hear when the snow begins to melt on twigs, branches, the roofs of houses, grass and pavements. What happens to icicles, to ice in gutters or on ponds, to slides and toboggan runs, to snowmen?

If you feel able to write a poem about the thaw, you may want to include several of these details in a general description, or concentrate on one feature, such as the icicle or the snowman.

5 Fog, like snow, makes familiar things seem unreal. It affects all our senses. What do you notice about the appearance of tall buildings, trees, street-lights, traffic, shop-windows, people? How are you aware of fog through the other senses of smell, sound, taste and touch?

The poem about fog on p. 128 likens the movement of the fog to that of a cat. Can you think of any comparisons to describe the movement and colour of fog?

DREAMS

The Very Image

An image of my grandmother
her head appearing upside-down upon a cloud
the cloud transfixed on the steeple
of a deserted railway-station
far away

An image of an aqueduct
with a dead crow hanging from the first arch
a modern-style chair from the second
a fir-tree lodged in the third
and the whole scene sprinkled with snow

An image of the piano-tuner
with a basket of prawns on his shoulder
and a firescreen under his arm
his moustache made of clay-clotted twigs
and his cheeks daubed with wine

An image of an aeroplane
the propeller is rashers of bacon
the wings are of reinforced lard
the tail is made of paper-clips
the pilot is a wasp

An image of the painter
with his left hand in a bucket
and his right hand stroking a cat
as he lies in bed
with a stone beneath his head

And all these images
and many others
are arranged like waxworks
in model bird-cages
about six inches high.

DAVID GASCOYNE

Nightmare

When you're lying awake with a dismal headache, and repose is taboo'd by anxiety,
I conceive you may use any language you choose to indulge in, without impropriety;
For your brain is on fire – the bedclothes conspire of usual slumber to plunder you:
First your counterpane goes, and uncovers your toes, and your sheet slips demurely from under you;
Then the blanketing tickles – you feel like mixed pickles – so terribly sharp is the pricking,
And you're hot, and you're cross, and you tumble and toss till there's nothing 'twixt you and the ticking.
Then the bedclothes all creep to the ground in a heap, and you pick 'em all up in a tangle;
Next your pillow resigns and politely declines to remain at its usual angle!

Well, you get some repose in the form of a doze, with hot eyeballs, and head ever aching,
But your slumbering teems with such horrible dreams that you'd very much better be waking;
For you dream you are crossing the Channel, and tossing about in a steamer from Harwich –
Which is something between a large bathing machine and a very small second-class carriage –
And you're giving a treat (penny ice and cold meat) to a party of friends and relations –
They're a ravenous horde – and they all came on board at Sloane Square and South Kensington Stations.
And bound on that journey you find your attorney (who started that morning from Devon);
He's a bit undersized, and you don't feel surprised when he tells you he's only eleven.
Well, you're driving like mad with this singular lad (by-the-bye the ship's now a four-wheeler),
And you're playing round games, and he calls you bad names when you tell him that 'ties pay the dealer';
But this you can't stand, so you throw up your hand, and you find you're as cold as an icicle,
In your shirt and your socks (the black silk with gold clocks), crossing Salisbury Plain on a bicycle:
And he and the crew are on bicycles too – which they've somehow or other invested in –
And he's telling the tars, all the particu*lars* of a company he's interested in –
It's a scheme of devices, to get at low prices, all goods from cough mixtures to cables
(Which tickled the sailors) by treating retailers, as though they were all vege*ta*bles –
You get a good spadesman to plant a small tradesman (first take off his boots with a boot-tree),
And his legs will take root, and his fingers will shoot, and they'll blossom and bud like a fruit-tree –

From the greengrocer tree you get grapes and green pea, cauliflower, pineapple, and cranberries,
While the pastrycook plant, cherry brandy will grant, apple puffs, and three-corners, and banberries –
The shares are a penny, and ever so many are taken by ROTHSCHILD and BARING,
And just as a few are allotted to you, you awake with a shudder despairing –
You're a regular wreck, with a crick in your neck, and no wonder you snore, for your head's on the floor, and you've needles and pins from your soles to your shins, and your flesh is a-creep for your left leg's asleep, and you've cramp in your toes, and a fly on your nose, and some fluff in your lung, and a feverish tongue, and a thirst that's intense, and a general sense that you haven't been sleeping in clover;
But the darkness has passed, and it's daylight at last, and the night has been long – ditto ditto my song – and thank goodness they're both of them over!

W. S. GILBERT

Kubla Khan

In Xanadu did Kubla Khan
A stately pleasure-dome decree:
Where Alph, the sacred river, ran
Through caverns measureless to man
  Down to a sunless sea.
So twice five miles of fertile ground
With walls and towers were girdled round:
And there were gardens bright with sinuous rills,
Where blossomed many an incense-bearing tree;
And here were forests ancient as the hills,
Enfolding sunny spots of greenery.

But oh! that deep romantic chasm which slanted
Down the green hill athwart a cedarn cover!
A savage place! as holy and enchanted
As e'er beneath a waning moon was haunted
By woman wailing for her demon-lover!
And from this chasm, with ceaseless turmoil seething,
As if this earth in fast thick pants were breathing,
A mighty fountain momently was forced:
Amid whose swift half-intermitted burst
Huge fragments vaulted like rebounding hail,
Or chaffy grain beneath the thresher's flail:
And 'mid these dancing rocks at once and ever
It flung up momently the sacred river.
Five miles meandering with a mazy motion
Through wood and dale the sacred river ran,
Then reached the caverns measureless to man,
And sank in tumult to a lifeless ocean:
And 'mid this tumult Kubla heard from far
Ancestral voices prophesying war!

The shadow of the dome of pleasure
Floated midway on the waves;
Where was heard the mingled measure
From the fountain and the caves.
It was a miracle of rare device,
A sunny pleasure-dome with caves of ice!

A damsel with a dulcimer
In a vision once I saw:
It was an Abyssinian maid,
And on her dulcimer she played,
Singing of Mount Abora.
Could I revive within me
Her symphony and song,
To such a deep delight 'twould win me,
That with music loud and long,
I would build that dome in air,

That sunny dome! those caves of ice!
And all who heard should see them there,
And all should cry, Beware! Beware!
His flashing eyes, his floating hair!
Weave a circle round him thrice,
And close your eyes with holy dread,
For he on honey-dew hath fed,
And drunk the milk of Paradise.

S. T. COLERIDGE

Portrait of a Boy

After the whipping, he crawled into bed;
Accepting the harsh fact with no great weeping.
How funny uncle's hat had looked striped red!
He chuckled silently. The moon came, sweeping
A black frayed rug of tattered cloud before
In scorning; very pure and pale she seemed,
Flooding his bed with radiance. On the floor
Fat motes danced. He sobbed; closed his eyes and dreamed.

Warm sand flowed round him. Blurts of crimson light
Splashed the white grains like blood. Past the cave's mouth
Shone with a large fierce splendour, wildly bright,
The crooked constellations of the South;
Here the Cross swung; and there, confronting Mars,
The Centaur stormed aside a froth of stars.
Within, great casks like wattled aldermen
Sighed of enormous feasts, and cloth of gold
Glowed on the walls like hot desire. Again
Beside webbed purples from some galleon's hold,
A black chest bore the skull and bones in white
Above a scrawled 'Gunpowder!' By the flames,

Decked out in crimson, gemmed with syenite,
Hailing their fellows by outrageous names
The pirates sat and diced. Their eyes were moons.
'Doubloons!' they said. The words crashed gold. 'Doubloons!'

STEPHEN VINCENT BENET

The Ice-cart

Perched on my city office-stool
I watched with envy while a cool
And lucky carter handled ice. . . .

And I was wandering in a trice
Far from the grey and grimy heat
Of that intolerable street
O'er sapphire berg and emerald floe
Beneath the still cold ruby glow
Of everlasting Polar night,
Bewildered by the queer half-light,
Until I stumbled unawares
Upon a creek where big white bears
Plunged headlong down with flourished heels
And floundered after shining seals
Through shivering seas of blinding blue.
And, as I watched them, ere I knew,
I'd stripped and I was swimming too
Among the seal-pack, young and hale,
And thrusting on with threshing tail,
With twist and twirl and sudden leap
Through crackling ice and salty deep,
Diving and doubling with my kind
Until at last we left behind
Those big white blundering bulks of death,
And lay at length with panting breath

Upon a far untravelled floe
Beneath a gentle drift of snow –
Snow drifting gently fine and white
Out of the endless Polar night,
Falling and falling evermore
Upon that far untravelled shore
Till I was buried fathoms deep
Beneath that cold white drifting sleep –
Sleep drifting deep,
Deep drifting sleep. . . .

The carter cracked a sudden whip:
I clutched my stool with startled grip,
Awakening to the grimy heat
Of that intolerable street.

WILFRID GIBSON

The Nightmare

Once, as in the darkness I lay asleep by night,
Strange things suddenly saw I in my dream;
All my dream was of monsters that came about me while I slept,
Devils and demons, four-horned, serpent-necked,
Fishes with bird-tails, three-legged bogies
From six eyes staring; dragons hideous,
Yet three-part human.
On rushed the foul flocks, grisly legions,
Stood round me, stretched out their arms,
Danced their hands about me, and sought to snatch me from my bed.
Then I cried (and in my dream
My voice was thick with anger and my words all awry),

'Ill-spawned elves, how dare you
Beset with your dire shapes Creation's cleanest
Shapeliest creature, Man?' Then straightway I struck out,
Flashed my fists like lightning among them, thumped like thunder,
Here slit Jack-o'-Lantern,
Here smashed fierce Hog-Face,
Battered wights and goblins,

Smote venturous vampires, pounded in the dust
Imps, gnomes and lobs,
Kobolds and kelpies;
Swiped bulge-eyed bogies, oafs and elves;
Clove Tough-head's triple skull, threw down
Clutching Night-hag, flogged the gawky Ear-wig Fiend
That floundered toward me on its tail.

I struck at staring eyes,
Stamped on upturned faces; through close ranks
Of hoofs I cut my way, buried my fingers deep
In half-formed flesh;
Ghouls tore at my touch; I slit sharp noses,
Trod on red tongues, seized shaggy manes,
Shook bald-heads by the beard.
Then was a scuffling. Arms and legs together
Chasing, crashing and sliding; a helter-skelter
Of feet lost and found in the tugging and toppling,
Cuffing, cudgelling, frenzied flogging . . .

So fought I, till terror and dismay
Shook those foul flocks; panic spread like a flame
Down mutinous ranks; they stand, they falter,
Those ghastly legions; but fleeing, suddenly turn
Glazed eyes upon me, to see how now I fare.
At last, to end their treachery
Again I rushed upon them, braved their slaver and snares,
Stood on a high place, and lashed down among them,
Shrieking and cursing as my blows crashed.

Then three by three and four by four
One after another hop-a-trot they fled,
Bellowing and bawling till the air was full of their breath –
Grumbling and snarling,
Those vanquished ogres, demons discomfited,
Some that would fain have run
Lolling and lurching, some that for cramped limbs
Could not stir from where they stood. Some over belly-wounds
Bent double; some in agony gasping and groaning.
Suddenly the clouds broke and (I knew not why)
A thin light filtered the darkness; then, while again
I sighed in wonder that those disastrous creatures,
Dire monstrosities, should dare assail
A clean and comely man, . . . there sounded in my ears
A twittering and crowing. And outdoors it was light.

The noisy cock, mindful that dawn was in the sky,
Had crowed his warning, and the startled ghosts,
Because they heard dawn heralded, had fled
In terror and tribulation from the rising day.

WANG YEN-SHOU
(Translated by Arthur Waley)

'Who's in the Next Room?'

'Who's in the next room? – who?
I seemed to see
Somebody in the dawning passing through,
Unknown to me.'
'Nay: you saw nought. He passed invisibly.'

'Who's in the next room? – who?
I seem to hear
Somebody muttering firm in a language new
That chills ear.'
'No: you catch not his tongue who has entered there.'
'Who's in the next room? – who?
I seem to feel
His breath like a clammy draught, as if it drew
From the Polar Wheel.'
'No: none who breathes at all does the door conceal.'

'Who's in the next room? – who?
A figure wan
With a message to one in there of something due?
Shall I know him anon?'
'Yea he; and he brought such; and you'll know him anon.'

THOMAS HARDY

Haunted

Evening was in the wood, louring with storm.
A time of drought had sucked the weedy pool
And baked the channels; birds had done with song.
Thirst was a dream of fountains in the moon,
Or willow-music blown across the water
Leisurely sliding on by weir and mill.

Uneasy was the man who wandered, brooding,
His face a little whiter than the dusk.
A drone of sultry wings flicker'd in his head.

The end of sunset burning thro' the boughs
Died in a smear of red; exhausted hours
Cumber'd, and ugly sorrows hemmed him in.

He thought: 'Somewhere there's thunder,' as he strove
To shake off dread; he dared not look behind him,
But stood, the sweat of horror on his face.

He blunder'd down a path, trampling on thistles,
In sudden race to leave the ghostly trees.
And: 'Soon I'll be in open fields,' he thought,
And half remembered starlight on the meadows,
Scent of mown grass and voices of tired men,
Fading along the field-paths; home and sleep
And cool-swept upland spaces, whispering leaves,
And far off the long churring night-jar's note.

But something in the wood, trying to daunt him,
Led him confused in circles through the thicket.
He was forgetting his old wretched folly,
And freedom was his need; his throat was choking.
Barbed brambles gripped and clawed him round his legs,
And he floundered over snags and hidden stumps.

Mumbling: 'I will get out! I must get out!'
Butting and thrusting up the baffling gloom,
Pausing to listen in a space 'twixt thorns,
He peers around with peering, frantic eyes.

An evil creature in the twilight looping,
Flapped blindly in his face. Beating it off,
He screeched in terror, and straightway something clambered
Heavily from an oak, and dropped, bent double,
To shamble at him zigzag, squat and bestial.

Headlong he charges down the wood, and falls
With roaring brain – agony – the snap't spark –
And blots of green and purple in his eyes.
Then the slow fingers groping on his neck,
And at his heart the strangling clasp of death.

SIEGFRIED SASSOON

Creative Writing

Most of you will dream or day-dream. Before you think about writing, you will find it helpful and interesting to spend some time talking about your dreams.

—Do you dream often or only at particular times when things out of the ordinary are happening – before examinations, or when you are ill?
—Are there some things which happen repeatedly in your dreams?
—How do your dreams end?
—Do you dream in colour or black and white?
—What role do you have most often? the hero? the villain? the bystander?
—Where do the subjects of your dreams come from? Your own recent experience? Things that happened years ago? Television?
—Have you ever had prophetic dreams?

What are the most vivid and frightening things about your nightmares?

Writing about dreams, day-dreams, or imaginary fears can be a strange and interesting business. Dreams, especially, are illogical; people and places come and go without reason or explanation; and often scenes change with great rapidity – like film shots 'dissolving' quickly. When you are writing, try to capture the dream effects: do not feel that you have to explain everything.

1 Write a poem about your most vivid dream or nightmare. The nightmarish picture of Medusa on p. 146 may set your imagination working.

2 Most people day-dream at one time or another and many of you will agree that school is a good place to do it! Why not put your day-dreams to some use by writing about them? *The Ice-cart* by W. W. Gibson on p. 144 is a good example of a day-dream poem. Start your poem in the real world: you may be at home, or school, or travelling on a bus or train with nothing to do; then let your poem wander into your dream-world until something happens to jolt you out of it.

3 Siegfried Sassoon's poem *Haunted* on p. 150 describes a man in the grip of an imaginary fear. Again, such fears are commonplace, but to the individual at the time they can be spine-chilling. Often they are associated with darkness. If you have experienced such fears perhaps you would write a poem about them, or about one of the following:

(i) walking home after dark
(ii) walking through woods on a windy night
(iii) my bedroom when it's dark
(iv) the feeling that someone is following me.

4 Look carefully at the photograph of Salvador Dali's painting, *Apparition of a Face and a Fruit Dish on a Beach*, on p. 138. What is dream-like about it? Are there any things which you cannot identify exactly, or which seem to change as you look at them?

Imagine yourself on the beach (*is* it a beach?) and write a poem describing what you see as you begin to walk towards the hills (*are* they hills?).

Alternatively, you could write a poem to describe your own dream-landscape where you find scenes and people strangely altered.

PEOPLE AND PLACES

Vista

A clatter of geese
fantastically waddling
over the jade silk lawn.

Behind them dark trees
genii clad in a green smoke
of leaves.

Under the trees,
warm and silent,
the mysterious, placid colours
of rhododendrons burn,
faintly,
electric blossoms,
like calm, pale,
subaqueous coral, . . . anemones.

Beyond,
stretching into sightless, unknown regions,
up the slope of a summitless hill,
a vista of low, contorted trees,
under a lavender sky.

What secret is hidden
at the end of the avenue?
A temple?
An iron gate?
A fragrant wilderness with briars?

DAVID GASCOYNE

My Parents Kept Me

My parents kept me from children who were rough
Who threw words like stones and who wore torn clothes.
Their thighs showed through rags. They ran in the street
And climbed cliffs and stripped by the country streams.

I feared more than tigers their muscles like iron
Their jerking hands and their knees tight on my arms.

I feared the salt coarse pointing of those boys
Who copied my lisp behind me on the road.

They were lithe, they sprang out behind hedges
Like dogs to bark at my world. They threw mud
While I looked the other way, pretending to smile.
I longed to forgive them, but they never smiled.

STEPHEN SPENDER

Lollocks

By sloth on sorrow fathered,
These dusty-featured Lollocks
Have their nativity in all disordered
Backs of cupboard drawers.

They play hide and seek
Among collars and novels
And empty medicine bottles,
And letters from abroad
That never will be answered.

Every sultry night
They plague little children,
Gurgling from the cistern,
Humming from the air,
Skewing up the bed-clothes,
Twitching the blind.

When the imbecile agèd
Are over-long in dying
And the nurse drowses,
Lollocks come skipping
Up the tattered stairs
And are nasty together
In the bed's shadow.

The signs of their presence
Are boils on the neck,
Dreams of vexation suddenly recalled
In the middle of the morning,
Languor after food.

Men cannot see them,
Men cannot hear them,
Do not believe in them –
But suffer the more
Both in neck and belly.

Women can see them –
O those naughty wives
Who sit by the fireside
Munching bread and honey,
Watching them in mischief
From corners of their eyes,
Slily allowing them to lick
Honey-sticky fingers.

Sovereign against Lollocks
Are hard broom and soft broom,
To well comb the hair,
To well brush the shoe,
And to pay every debt
As it falls due.

ROBERT GRAVES

Mole Catcher

With a coat like any mole's, as soft and black,
And hazel bows bundled beneath his arm,
With long-helved spade and rush bag on his back,
The trapper plods alone about the farm:
And spies new mounds in the ripe pasture-land,
And where the lob-worms writhe up in alarm
And easy sinks the spade, he takes his stand
Knowing the moles' dark high-road runs below:
Then sharp and square he chops the turf, and day
Gloats on the opened turnpike through the clay.

Out from his wallet hurry pin and prong,
And trap, and noose to tie it to the bow;
And then his grand arcanum, oily and strong,
Found out by his forefather years ago
To scent the peg and witch the moles along.
The bow is earthed and arched ready to shoot
And snatch the death-knot fast round the first mole
Who comes and snuffs well pleased and tries to root
Past the sly nose peg; back again is put
The mould, and death left smirking in the hole.
The old man goes and tallies all his snares
And finds the prisoners there and takes his toll.

And moles to him are only moles; but hares
See him afield and scarcely cease to nip
Their dinners, for he harms not them; he spares
The drowning fly that of his ale would sip
And throws the ant the crumbs of comradeship.
And every time he comes into his yard
Grey linnet knows he brings the groundsel sheaf,
And clatters round the cage to be unbarred,
And on his finger whistles twice as hard. –
What his old vicar says, is his belief,
In the side pew he sits and hears the truth;
And never misses once to ring his bell
On Sundays night and morn, nor once since youth
Has heard the chimes afield, but has heard tell
There's not a peal in England sounds so well.

EDMUND BLUNDEN

In a Sailplane

Still as a bird
Transfixed in flight
We shiver and flow
Into leagues of light.

Rising and turning
Without a sound
As summer lifts us
Off the ground.

The sky's deep bell
Of glass rings down.
We slip in a sea
That cannot drown.

We kick the wide
Horizon's blues
Like a cluttering hoop
From round our shoes.

This easy 'plane
So quietly speaks,
Like a tree it sighs
In silvery shrieks.

Neatly we soar
Through a roaring cloud:
Its caverns of snow
Are dark and loud.

Into banks of sun
Above the drifts
Of quilted cloud
Our stillness shifts.

Here no curious
Bird comes near.
We float alone
In a snowman's sphere.

Higher than spires
Where breath is rare
We beat the shires
Of racing air.

Up the cliff
Of sheer no-place
We swarm a rope
That swings on space.

Breezed by a star's
Protracted stare
We watch the earth
Drop out of air.

Red stars of light
Burn on the round
Of land: street-constellations
Strew the ground.

Their bridges leap
From town to town:
Into lighted dusk
We circle down.

Still as a bird
Transfixed in flight
We come to nest
In the field of night.

JAMES KIRKUP

Hunter Trials

It's awfully bad luck on Diana,
  Her ponies have swallowed their bits;
She fished down their throats with a spanner
  And frightened them all into fits.

So now she's attempting to borrow.
  Do lend her some bits, Mummy, *do*;
I'll lend her my own for tomorrow.
  But to-day *I'll* be wanting them too.

Just look at Prunella on Guzzle;
  The wizardest pony on earth;
Why doesn't she slacken his muzzle
  And tighten the breech in his girth?

I say, Mummy, there's Mrs. Geyser
  And doesn't she look pretty sick?
I bet it's because Mona Lisa
  Was hit on the hock with a brick.

Miss Blewitt says Monica threw it,
  But Monica says it was Joan,
And Joan's very thick with Miss Blewitt,
  So Monica's sulking alone.

And Margaret failed in her paces,
  Her withers got tied in a noose,
So her coronet's caught in the traces
  And now all her fetlocks are loose.

Oh, it's me now. I'm terribly nervous.
  I wonder if Smudges will shy.
She's practically certain to swerve as
  Her Pelham is over one eye.

* * *

Oh, wasn't it naughty of Smudges?
  Oh, Mummy, I'm sick with disgust.
She threw me in front of the Judges,
  And my silly old collarbone's bust.

JOHN BETJEMAN

I Know Some Lonely Houses off the Road

I know some lonely houses off the road
A robber'd like the look of, –
Wooden barred,
And windows hanging low,
Inviting to
A portico,

Where two could creep:
One hand the tools,
The other peep
To make sure all's asleep.
Old-fashioned eyes,
Not easy to surprise!

How orderly the kitchen'd look by night,
With just a clock, –
But they could gag the tick,
And mice won't bark;
And so the walls don't tell,
None will.

A pair of spectacles ajar just stir –
An almanac's aware.
Was it the mat winked,
Or a nervous star?
The moon slides down the stair
To see who's there.

There's plunder, – where?
Tankard, or spoon,
Earring, or stone,
A watch, some ancient brooch
To match the grandmamma,
Staid sleeping there.

Day rattles, too,
Stealth's slow;
The sun has got as far
As the third sycamore.
Screams chanticleer,
'Who's there?'

And echoes, trains away,
Sneer – 'Where?'
While the old couple, just astir,
Think that the sunrise left the door ajar!

EMILY DICKINSON

Fishing Harbour towards Evening

Slashed clouds leak gold. Along the slurping wharf
The snugged boats creak and seesaw. Round the masts

Abrasive squalls flake seagulls off the sky:
Choppy with wings the rapids of shrill sound.

Wrapt in spliced airs of fish and tar,
Light wincing on their knives, the clockwork men

Incise and scoop the oily pouches, flip
The soft guts overboard with blood-wet fingers.

Among three rhythms the slapping silver turns
To polished icy marble upon the deck.

RICHARD KELL

The Bridge

Out of the silence grows
An iron thunder – grows, and roars, and sweeps,
Menacing. The plain
Suddenly leaps,
Startled, from its repose –
Alert and listening. Now from the gloom
Of the soft distance loom
Three lights and, over them, a brush

Of tawny flame and flying spark –
Three pointed lights that rush,
Monstrous, upon the cringing dark.
And nearer, nearer rolls the sound,
Louder the throb and roar of wheels,
The shout of speed, the shriek of steam;
The slope of bank,
Cut into flashing squares, gives back the clank
And grind of metal, while the ground
Shudders and the bridge reels –
As, with a scream,
The train
A rage of smoke, a laugh of fire,
A lighted anguish of desire,
A dream
Of gold and iron, of sound and flight,
Tumultuous roars across the night.

J. REDWOOD ANDERSON

Morning Glory

My father would begin each day
By standing in the backyard door
And giving one tremendous sneeze,
Mid-way between a gasp and roar:

Would clap a fist before his eyes,
And give a kind of stamping dance,
As if his spirit wept and sang
To hear such goodly resonance.

And even now I can remember
His gaiters, and the scads of mire
He kicked before him, as this greeting
Sprang from his nostrils like a fire.

And cocks in every neighbouring yard
Would lift their heads, and strut and stir,
Sensing the challenge of some odd,
Irate and twanging chanticlere.

MICHELL RAPER

Morning at the Window

They are rattling breakfast plates in basement kitchens.
And along the trampled edges of the street
I am aware of the damp souls of housemaids
Sprouting despondently at area gates.

The brown waves of fog toss up to me
Twisted faces from the bottom of the street,
And tear from a passer-by with muddy skirts
An aimless smile that hovers in the air
And vanishes along the level of the roofs.

T. S. ELIOT

From Tattooed

On his arm he wears
Diagrams he chose,
A snake inside a skull.
A dagger in a rose,

And the muscle playing
Under the skin
Makes the rose writhe
And the skull grin.

WILLIAM PLOMER

The Unfortunate Miller

On windy days the mill
Turned with a will,
But on calm days it spread
Its four sails – dead.

The one-eyed miller man
Laments that ban,
And to the windless sky
Turning his vexed eye:

'God help,' he sadly says,
'This business;
A hundred days and more
The wind's forebore,

And lacking breezes I
Am bound to die;
The profit I've forgone
In offal and grist alone

Would have bought a cock and a hen,
A gilt for my pen,
And a row of asters planted
Just where I wanted;

But since the wind is still –
The devil take the mill!
Never it rains but pours –
Let's in-a-doors.'

So in-a-doors goes he
To see – alas, to see –
Not the scrapings of a pan or pot
In his famished cot.

The tap of the clock indoors,
The dusty floors,
His empty crock and purse,
Made bad seem worse.

He looked at himself in the glass –
How thin he was!
He looked at the time and date –
Too late! Too late!

And creeping again to the mill
That stood stone still,
He tied round his neck the loop
Of a long dark rope,

Drove a tenpenny nail
Into the mill's black sail,
Hung his watch on a shelf,
Then hung himself.

And lo, the wind came! Beshrew,
How the wind blew!
And the sails, with the miller dying,
Went flying, flying.

A. E. COPPARD

Thrushes

The City Financier
walks in the gardens
stiffly, because of
his pride and his burdens.

The daisies, looking
up, observe
only a self-
respecting curve.

The thrushes only
see a flat
table-land
of shiny hat.

He looks importantly
about him,
while all the spring
goes on without him.

HUMBERT WOLFE

Eight o'Clock

He stood, and heard the steeple
  Sprinkle the quarters on the morning town.
One, two, three, four, to market-place and people
  It tossed them down.

Strapped, noosed, nighing his hour,
  He stood and counted them and cursed his luck;
And then the clock collected in the tower
  Its strength, and struck.

A. E. HOUSMAN

Roman Wall Blues

Over the heather the wet wind blows,
I've lice in my tunic and a cold in my nose.

The rain comes pattering out of the sky,
I'm a Wall soldier, I don't know why.

The mist creeps over the hard grey stone,
My girl's in Tungria; I sleep alone.

Aulus goes hanging around her place,
I don't like his manners, I don't like his face.

Piso's a Christian, he worships a fish;
There'd be no kissing if he had his wish.

She gave me a ring but I diced it away;
I want my girl and I want my pay.

When I'm a veteran with only one eye
I shall do nothing but look at the sky.

W. H. AUDEN

Old Furniture

I know not how it may be with others
  Who sit among relics of householdry
That date from the days of their mothers' mothers,
  But well I know how it is with me
    Continually.

I see the hands of the generations
  That owned each shiny familiar thing
In play on its knobs and indentations,
  And with its ancient fashioning
    Still dallying:

Hands behind hands, growing paler and paler,
  As in a mirror a candle-flame
Shows images of itself, each frailer
  As it recedes, though the eye may frame
    Its shape the same.

On the clock's dull dial a foggy finger,
  Moving to set the minutes right
With tentative touches that lift and linger
  In the wont of a moth on a summer night,
    Creeps to my sight.

On this old viol, too, fingers are dancing –
  As whilom – just over the strings by the nut,
The tip of a bow receding, advancing
  In airy quivers, as if it would cut
    The plaintive gut.

And I see a face by that box for tinder,
  Glowing forth in fits from the dark,
And fading again as the linten cinder
  Kindles to red at the flinty spark,
    Or goes out stark.

Well, well. It is best to be up and doing,
  The world has no use for one today
Who eyes things thus – no aim pursuing!
  He should not continue in this stay,
    But sink away.

THOMAS HARDY

Things Men Have Made

Things men have made with wakened hands, and put soft life into
are awake through years with transferred touch, and go on glowing
for long years.
And for this reason, some old things are lovely
warm still with the life of forgotten men who made them.

D. H. LAWRENCE

Creative Writing

1 Most of you will have a favourite place where you play or which you visit on holidays or at weekends. The boys in the photograph on p. 154 have, perhaps, found such a place. Where and how do you like to spend your spare time? Perhaps you could write about it.

2 Airports, stations, ports and harbours are all 'in-between' places. They have a strange atmosphere, perhaps because no-one seems to belong there; everyone is just passing through. If you have had this feeling, try to write about it.

3 Most of you, at some time, will have been alone in a group of people, all of them complete strangers to you. You may have been travelling on a bus or train or waiting in a queue for the cinema or football match. Perhaps you have wondered who they are, what they do for a living, where they live and so on. If you have ever passed the time in this way, you may feel able to write a poem about it.

4 Some of you will know an old man or woman who has little interest in life other than sitting at a front window watching the life of the street pass by. Either, write a poem which describes how you see him or her, or one which sets down the stream of thoughts, feelings and memories which go through this person's mind.

5 Near your home there may well be a row of shops where your mother usually sends you to do the errands. Perhaps you know the inside of the shops, the shop-keepers and the customers quite well. Try to write a poem describing the things or people you find most interesting when shopping locally.

You might, for example, prefer to concentrate on one particular shop – its contents, atmosphere, colours, shapes, sounds – or on one particular shop-keeper.

Alternatively, you may want to contrast the butcher's with the milliner's, or a traditional small shop with the modern supermarket.

You will find a different atmosphere in an open street-market. L. S. Lowry's picture on p. 158 may suggest a poem to you.

6 The photograph on p. 39 appeared on the front page of *Pravda* captioned, 'Up to space – this picture was taken when the

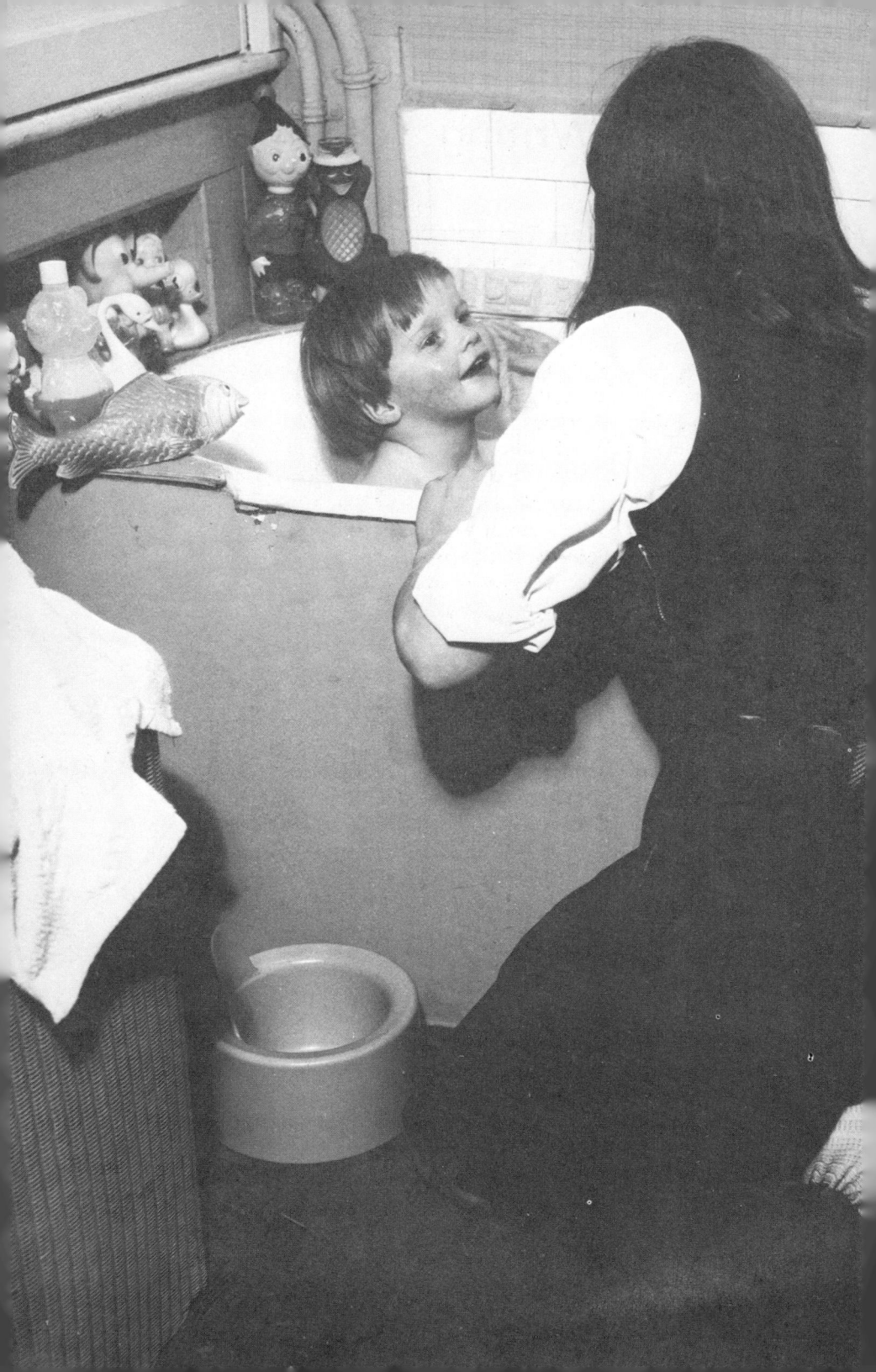

rocket came from the clouds – photographed by Valentin Lebedev.' The caption did not say how, where or when.

The photograph may help you to imagine what spaceflight is like and you may be able to write a poem describing not only the things you see – clouds, planets, the world from space – but also the feelings of an astronaut during countdown, blast-off and orbit.

Alternatively, you could imagine this rocket on its way to the moon and describe the last few minutes before touchdown as the unfamiliar moonscape looms closer.

7 Many of you will have younger sisters or brothers. Sometimes your mother may ask you to help in looking after them: you may find yourself pushing the pram, bathing the baby, reading stories, playing games. On p. 178 there is a photograph of a girl of thirteen bathing her younger sister. The picture is attractive largely because it shows so many details of ordinary life – the toys, the towel draped over the clothes basket, the rolled-up sleeve, the potty. The photograph may set you thinking of times when you have helped about the house and you may be able to write about one of them. Whatever you choose, try to capture everyday details.

8 The photograph on p. 168 shows a street-corner scene which may remind you of bleak, wintry days in town. Can you find words to describe the way snow sticks to coats, road-signs and pillars and affects roads and pavements? What do you notice about the way people stand? What details tell you that there is a strong wind driving the snow? What do you imagine the people's feelings to be? You may be able to write a poem suggested by the picture.

TOWN AND COUNTRY

Flat Suburbs, S.W., in the Morning

The new red houses spring like plants
  In level rows
Of reddish herbage that bristles and slants
  Its square shadows.

The pink young houses show one side bright
  Flatly assuming the sun,
And one side shadow, half in sight,
  Half-hiding the pavement-run;

Where hastening creatures pass intent
  On their level way,
Threading like ants that can never relent
  And have nothing to say.

Bare stems of street lamps stiffly stand
  At random, desolate twigs,
To testify to a blight on the land
  That has stripped their sprigs.

D. H. LAWRENCE

Let Us Be Men

For God's sake, let us be men
not monkeys minding machines
or sitting with our tails curled
while the machine amuses us, the radio or film or gramophone.

Monkeys with a bland grin on our faces.

D. H. LAWRENCE

The Manor Farm

The rock-like mud unfroze a little and rills
Ran and sparkled down each side of the road
Under the catkins wagging in the hedge.
But earth would have her sleep out, spite of the sun;
Nor did I value that thin gilding beam
More than a pretty February thing
Till I came down to the old Manor Farm,
And church and yew-tree opposite, in age
Its equals and in size. The church and yew
And farmhouse slept in a Sunday silentness.
The air raised not a straw. The steep farm roof,
With tiles duskily glowing, entertained
The mid-day sun; and up and down the roof
White pigeons nestled. There was no sound but one.
Three cart-horses were looking over a gate
Drowsily through their forelocks, swishing their tails
Against a fly, a solitary fly.

The Winter's cheek flushed as if he had drained
Spring, Summer, and Autumn at a draught
And smiled quietly. But 'twas not Winter –

Rather a season of bliss unchangeable
Awakened from farm and church where it had lain
Safe under tile and thatch for ages since
This England, Old already, was called Merry.

EDWARD THOMAS

The Beech

Strength leaves the hand I lay on this beech-bole
  So great-girthed, old and high;
Its sprawling arms like iron serpents roll
  Between me and the sky.

One elbow on the sloping earth it leans,
  That steeply falls beneath,
As though resting a century it means
  To take a moment's breath.

Its long thin buds in glistering varnish dipt
  Are swinging up and down
While one young beech that winter left unstript
  Still wears its withered crown.

At least gust of the wind the great tree heaves
  From heavy twigs to groin;
The wind sighs as it rakes among dead leaves
  For some lost key or coin.

And my blood shivers as away it sweeps
  Rustling the leaves that cling
Too late to that young withered beech that keeps
  Its autumn in the spring.

ANDREW YOUNG

Throwing a Tree

The two executioners stalk along over the knolls,
Bearing two axes with heavy heads shining and wide,
And a long limp two-handled saw toothed for cutting great boles,
And so they approach the proud tree that bears the death-mark on its side.

Jackets doffed they swing axes and chop away just above ground,
And the chips fly about and lie white on the moss and fallen leaves;
Till a broad deep gash in the bark is hewn all the way round,
And one of them tries to hook upward a rope, which at last he achieves.

The saw then begins, till the top of the tall giant shivers:
The shivers are seen to grow greater each cut than before:
They edge out the saw, tug the rope; but the tree only quivers,
And kneeling and sawing again, they step back to try pulling once more.

Then, lastly, the living mast sways, further sways: with a shout
Job and Ike rush aside. Reached the end of its long staying powers
The tree crashes downward: it shakes all its neighbours throughout,
And two hundred years' steady growth has been ended in less than two hours.

THOMAS HARDY

Root Cellar

Nothing would sleep in that cellar, dank as a ditch,
Bulbs broke out of boxes hunting for chinks in the dark,
Shoots dangled and drooped,
Lolling obscenely from mildewed crates,
Hung down long yellow evil necks, like tropical snakes.
And what a congress of stinks! –
Roots ripe as old bait,
Pulpy stems, rank, silo-rich,
Leaf-mould, manure, lime, piled against slippery planks.
Nothing would give up life:
Even the dirt kept breathing a small breath.

THEODORE ROETHKE

Digging

Today I think
Only with scents – scents dead leaves yield,
And bracken, and wild carrot's seed,
And the square mustard field;

Odours that rise
When the spade wounds the root of tree,
Rose, currant, raspberry, or goutweed,
Rhubarb or celery;

The smoke's smell, too,
Flowing from where a bonfire burns
The dead, the waste, the dangerous,
And all to sweetness turns.

It is enough
To smell, to crumble the dark earth,
While the robin sings over again
Sad songs of Autumn mirth.

EDWARD THOMAS

Summer Night

As we walk, the moon ahead of us
Appears to be falling through
Each tree we pass, and sieves
Star after star through screens
Of thickening leaves.

The green hedge is wider now
With white may, hanging grass. The chestnut
Trims itself with pink and snowy cones;
The moon as we walk drops through each tree
And scatters silvery grit among the country stones.

JAMES KIRKUP

The Winter Trees

Against the evening sky the trees are black,
Iron themselves against the iron rails;
The hurrying crowds seek cinemas or homes,
A cosy hour where warmth will mock the wind.
They do not look at the trees now summer's gone,
For fallen with the leaves are those glad days
Of sand and sea and ships, of swallows, lambs,
Of cricket teams, and walking long in woods.

Standing among the trees a shadow bends
And picks a cigarette-end from the ground;
It lifts the collar of an overcoat,
And blows upon its hands and stamps its feet –
For this is winter, chastiser of the free,
This is the winter, kind only to the bound.

CLIFFORD DYMENT

Creative Writing

1 Write a poem suggested by one of the following: the discovery of some eggs in a bird's nest; dragon-flies over a pond; wild flowers; the plumage of a bird's wing; a cat stalking a bird; climbing a tree; minnows and sticklebacks in a pool or stream; crawling through bracken; a nest of wasps or bees; dandelion clocks.

In all of these subjects you will need to look closely and concentrate hard on your imaginary picture. If you write about the last suggestion you will find the photograph on p. 184 helpful. Record the details carefully and try to find comparisons to help the reader *see* what you are describing.

2 Look again at D. H. Lawrence's poem about the London suburbs on p. 180. Notice how Lawrence picks out the details of his scene: the rows of houses, their colour, the shadows, the ant-like people, the street-lamps. . . . Many of the man-made objects are described as strange, unnatural plants – which helps us to understand Lawrence's feelings about them. If you live in suburbs you may recognise the sort of area he is describing and possibly share his attitude to it. But, wherever you live, you may be able to write about your own street.

Decide, first, what you really think of your area: the times of day when you like it, those when you don't; things you like and dislike about it, and then – when you have noted down some of the details and feelings you want to include – try to make your poem. You may want to use your road name as a title.

3 You may be able to write a poem suggested by one of the following: inside a heavy engineering factory or steelworks; a large power station or gasworks; engine sheds; a river or canal in the heart of an industrial city; your city centre.

4 Perhaps you have noticed that trees often have distinctive shapes. Try to jot down quickly one or two words, phrases and comparisons to describe the shape of one of the following: a poplar, a willow-tree, an oak, a pine-tree. Whichever tree you have chosen, now, look at it more closely.

What is the shape and design of its leaves?
What does the bark feel like to touch?
Are any of its roots visible? What are they like?
How does the tree move in the wind?

You may be able to write a poem which describes the outline and details of a particular tree.

Or, if you like, you could find a leaf which has an interesting shape, colour or surface pattern and try to describe it in detail. It might be helpful to press the leaf and put it in your book opposite the finished poem.

5 Arcimboldo's picture of *Summer* on p. 187 is certainly very strange. How many plants and fruits can you identify? You may be able to do in words what Arcimboldo has done in his painting and imagine, for example, Winter, Death, Time or the City in human form. You might see Winter as a bare tree, with branches for limbs and ice-covered twigs for fingers – there are lots of possibilities here.

Index of First Lines

A clatter of geese 153
After the long drought 126
After the whipping, he crawled into bed 143
Against the evening sky the trees are black 186
Against the stone breakwater 129
An image of my grandmother 136
As we walk, the moon ahead of us 186
At midnight in the alley 73
A yellowhammer in her mouth, the cat came mewing 67

Blood punches through every vein 40
By sloth on sorrow fathered 156

Climbing through the January snow, into the Lobo canyon 28
Come all you rounders if you want to hear 110
Cottonwool clouds loiter 134

Do you remember an Inn 55
Drum on your drums, batter on your banjoes 44

Evening was in the wood, louring with storm 150
Exploiter of the shadows 67

Fat black bucks in a wine-barrel room 60
For God's sake, let us be men 181
Forth from his den to steal he stole 118
Frost calls to water 'Halt!' 127
Fury said to 6

Heart aches 3
He stood, and heard the steeple 174

I don't know how many thousand years 34
I don't mind eels 119
I know not how it may be with others 175
I know some lonely houses off the road 165
In Just – 33
Insu nli gh t 30
In Xanadu did Kubla Khan 141
'I really take it very kind 115
I started early, took my dog 105
It is an ancient Mariner 83
It's awfully bad luck on Diana 163

jollymerry 36
Johnny Nolan has a patch on his ass 35

Look, stranger, at this island now 37

Molly Vickers 58
My father would begin each day 170
My parents kept me from the children who were rough 154

Nothing would sleep in that cellar, dank as a ditch 184
Now it is almost night, from the bronzey soft sky 129

Once, as in the darkness I lay asleep by night 145
One this snowflake 31
On his arm he wears 171
On lonely river-mud a heron alone 78
On windy days the mill 171
Out of the silence grows 167
Over the heather the wet wind blows 174
O what is that sound which so thrills the ear 53

Perched on my city office-stool 144

Rain 125
Raising my pen to put a point 76
Ridged thickly on black bough 132

Slashed clouds leak gold. Along the slurping wharf 166
Somebody is throttling that tree 131
Some primal termite knocked on wood 119
Still as a bird 161
Strength leaves the hands I lay on this beech-hole 182
Swart, swarthy smiths besmattered with smoke 43
Swift of foot was Hiawatha 122

Tell you I chyll 44
The apes yawn and adore their fleas in the sun 68
The City Financier 173
The firefly's flame 119
The five old bells 19
The fog comes 128
The heron stands in water where the swamp 78
The hunter crouches in his blind 119
The new red houses spring like plants 180
The rock-like mud unfroze a little and rills 181
The rustling of leaves under the feet in woods and under hedges 50
The sky's as blue and black as ink 7
The splendour falls on castle walls 48

The town is still 41
The two executioners stalk along over the knolls 183
There is the silence of a copse or croft 47
There's a snake on the western wave 106
There's a whisper down the line at 11.39 56
There was an old fellow of Tring 120
There was an old man from Darjeeling 120
There was an old man from Dunoon 120
There was a young man of Montrose 120
They are rattling breakfast plates in basement kitchens 170
They paddle with staccato feet 70
Things men have made with wakened hands, and put soft life into 176
This darksome burn, horseback brown 53
This is the night mail crossing the border 18
Tim Finnegan liv'd in Walkin Street 108
Tim Turpin he was gravel blind 112
Today I think 185
'Twas brillig, and the slithy toves 9
Twitching the leaves just where the drainpipe clogs 72
Two old Bachelors were living in one house 117
Tyger! Tyger! burning bright 69

We are going to see the rabbit 79
We spray the fields and scatter 121
What heart could have thought you? 32
When did you start your tricks 25
When he killed the Mudjokivis 123
When you're lying awake with a dismal headache 137
'Who called?' I said, and the words 48
'Who's in the next room?–who? 149
With a coat like any mole's, as soft and black 160

You wake, all windows blind – embattled sprays 126

Index of Authors

Anderson, J. Redwood 167
Anon 43, 108, 110, 118, 120, 123
Apollinaire, Guillaume 7
Auden, W. H. 18, 22, 37, 53, 174

Belloc, Hilaire 55
Benét, Stephen Vincent 143
Bennett, Arnold 120
Berry, Francis 41
Betjeman, John 121, 163
Blake, William 69
Blunden, Edmund 160
Brownjohn, Alan 79

Carroll, Lewis 6, 9
Clare, John 50
Coleridge, Samuel Taylor 83, 141
Connor, Tony 58
Coppard, A. E. 171
Cummings, E. E. 30, 31, 33

De la Mare, Walter 48
Dickinson, Emily 105, 165
Dyment, Clifford 67, 186

Eliot, T. S. 56, 170

Ferlinghetti, Lawrence 35

Gascoyne, David 136, 153
Gibson, Wilfrid 144
Gilbert, W. S. 137
Graves, Robert 156

Hardy, Thomas 47, 149, 175, 183
Heath-Stubbs, John 34, 74
Hesketh, Phoebe 78
Hood, Thomas 112, 115
Hopkins, G. M. 53
Housman, A. E. 174
Hughes, Ted 68
Hunt, Peter 8

Kell, Richard 70, 166
Kirkup, James 40, 126, 161, 186

Lawrence, D. H. 25, 28, 75, 129, 176, 180, 181
Lear, Edward 117
Levertov, Denise 76
Lindsay, Vachel 15, 60, 106
Longfellow, H. W. 122

Marquis, Don 73
Morgan, Edwin 36

Nash, Ogden 119
Nicholson, Norman 125
Noyce, Wilfrid 3

Plomer, William 171

Raper, Michell 170
Redgrove, Peter 131
Roethke, Theodore 78, 129, 184
Ross, Alan 76

Sandburg, Carl 46, 128
Sassoon, Siegfried 150
Skelton, John 44
Spender, Stephen 154

Tennyson, Lord 48
Tessimond, A. S. J. 134
Thomas, Edward 181, 185
Thompson, Francis 32
Thwaite, Anthony 72
Tomlinson, Charles 126

Wolfe, Humbert 173

Yen-Shou, Wang 145
Young, Andrew 127, 132, 182

Sources and Acknowledgements

Thanks are due to the authors (or their executors), their representatives and publishers mentioned in the following list for their kind permission to reproduce copyright material:

Wilfrid Noyce: 'Breathless' from *South Col*, William Heinemann Ltd.

G. Apollinaire: 'Calligram' from *Selected Poems*, Penguin Books Ltd.

W. H. Auden: 'Night Mail', 'On This Island', 'The Quarry' and 'Roman Wall Blues' from *Collected Shorter Poems 1927–1957*, Faber & Faber Ltd.

D. H. Lawrence: 'The Mosquito', 'Mountain Lion', 'Two Performing Elephants', 'Storm in the Black Forest', 'Things Men Have Made', 'Flat Suburbs, S.W., in the Morning' and 'Let Us Be Men' from *The Complete Poems of D. H. Lawrence*, Laurence Pollinger Ltd., and the Estate of the late Mrs. Frieda Lawrence.

E. E. Cummings: 'Insu nli gh t' and 'One' from *73 Poems* by E. E. Cummings, © 1963 by Marion Morehouse Cummings. Reprinted by permission of Harcourt, Brace & World Inc., and MacGibbon & Kee. 'In Just-spring', copyright 1923, 1951, by E. E. Cummings; reprinted from his volume *Poems 1923–1954* by permission of Harcourt, Brace & World Inc., and MacGibbon & Kee.

Lawrence Ferlinghetti: 'Johnny Nolan' from *A Coney Island of the Mind,* © 1958 by Lawrence Ferlinghetti. Reprinted by permission of Laurence Pollinger Ltd., and New Directions Publishing Corporation, New York.

Edwin Morgan: 'The Computer's First Christmas Card' from *Concrete Poetry*, London Magazine.

James Kirkup: 'Thunder and Lightning', 'Early Rain', 'In a Sailplane' and 'Summer Night' from *The Prodigal Son*, Oxford University Press.

Carl Sandburg: 'Jazz Fantasia' from *Smoke and Steel* by Carl Sandburg, © 1920 by Harcourt, Brace & World Inc. 'Fog' from *Chicago Poems*, © 1916 by Holt, Rinehart & Winston Inc. Copyright 1944 by Carl Sandburg. Reprinted by permission of Holt, Rinehart & Winston Inc., Publishers, New York, and Laurence Pollinger Ltd.

Walter de la Mare: 'Echo' from *Collected Poems*, the Literary Trustees of Walter de la Mare, and the Society of Authors.

G. M. Hopkins: 'Inversnaid' from *Collected Poems*, Oxford University Press.

Hilaire Belloc: 'Tarantella', reprinted by permission of A. D. Peters & Co.

Emily Dickinson: 'I Started Early' and 'I Know Some Lonely Houses off the Road', reprinted by permission of the publishers and the Trustees of Amherst College from Thomas H. Johnson, Editor, *The Poems of Emily Dickinson,* Cambridge, Mass., U.S.A.: The Belknap Press of Harvard University Press, copyright 1951, 1955, by the President and Fellows of Harvard College.

Norman Nicholson: 'Rain' from *The Pot Geranium*, Faber & Faber Ltd.

Charles Tomlinson: 'Winter Piece' from *A Peopled Landscape,* Oxford University Press.

Peter Redgrove: 'A Storm' from *The Collector*, Routledge & Kegan Paul Ltd.

A. S. J. Tessimond: 'A Hot Day' from *Selection*, Putnam and Hubert Nicholson.

David Gascoyne: 'The Very Image' from *Collected Poems*, Oxford University Press, and 'Vista'.

W. W. Gibson: 'The Ice-Cart' from *Collected Poems 1905–1925*, Mr Michael Gibson, The Macmillan Company of Canada Ltd., and Macmillan & Co. Ltd.

Wang Yen-Shou: 'The Nightmare' from *Chinese Poems*, translated by Arthur Waley, George Allen & Unwin Ltd.

Siegfried Sassoon: 'Haunted' from *Collected Poems,* the Executors of the late Siegfried Sassoon.

Robert Graves: 'Lollocks' from *Collected Poems 1965*, A. P. Watt & Son.

Stephen Spender: 'My Parents Kept Me from Children Who Were Rough' from *Collected Poems*, Faber & Faber Ltd.

Edmund Blunden: 'Mole Catcher' from *Poems of Many Years*, William Collins & Sons Ltd., reprinted by permission of A. D. Peters & Co.

J. Redwood Anderson: 'The Bridge' from *Walls and Hedges*, Sidgwick & Jackson Ltd.

Michell Raper: 'Morning Glory'.

William Plomer: the first two stanzas of 'Tattooed' from *Collected Poems,* Jonathan Cape Ltd.

A. E. Coppard: 'The Unfortunate Miller' from *Collected Poems*, Jonathan Cape Ltd., reprinted by permission of A. D. Peters & Co.

Humbert Wolfe: 'Thrushes', Miss Ann Wolfe.

Edward Thomas: 'Digging', Miss Myfanwy Thomas.

Francis Berry: 'Fall of a Tower' from *The Galloping Centaur,* Methuen & Co. Ltd.

T. S. Eliot: 'Morning at the Window' from *Collected Poems 1909–1962,* and 'Skimbleshanks: The Railway Cat' from *Old Possum's Book of Practical Cats,* Faber & Faber Ltd.

Clifford Dyment: 'Fox', 'Carrion' and 'Winter Trees' from *Poems 1935–1948*, J. M. Dent & Sons Ltd.

Ted Hughes: 'The Jaguar' from *The Hawk in the Rain*, Faber & Faber Ltd., and Harper & Row Inc., New York.

Richard Kell: 'Fishing Harbour Towards Evening' and 'Pigeons' from *Control Tower*, Chatto & Windus Ltd.

Anthony Thwaite: 'Hedgehog' from *The Owl in the Tree*, Oxford University Press.

Don Marquis: 'The Tom-Cat', copyright 1917 by Sun Printing and Publishing Association, from *Poems and Portraits* by Don Marquis. Reprinted by permission of Doubleday & Co. Inc.

Denise Levertov: 'The Disclosure' from *O Taste and See*, © by Denise Levertov Goodman, and reprinted by permission of New Directions Publishing Corporation, New York.

Theodore Roethke: 'Root Cellar', © 1943 by Modern Poetry Association Inc.; 'The Heron', © 1937 by Theodore Roethke; and 'The Storm', © 1961 by Beatrice Roethke as Administratrix of the Estate of Theodore Roethke; all from *The Collected Poems of Theodore Roethke*. Reprinted by permission of Doubleday & Co. Inc. 'Root Cellar' and 'The Heron', Martin Secker & Warburg Ltd. 'The Storm', Faber & Faber Ltd.

Alan Brownjohn: 'The Rabbit'.

Alan Ross: 'Death of a Fly' from *African Negatives*, Eyre & Spottiswoode (Publishers) Ltd.

Thomas Hardy: 'Silences', 'Who's in the Next Room?', 'Throwing a Tree' and 'Old Furniture' from *The Collected Poems of Thomas Hardy*, the Trustees of the Hardy Estate, Macmillan & Co. Ltd., and the Macmillan Company of Canada.

Ogden Nash: 'The Hunter', 'The Eel', 'The Termite' and 'The Firefly' from *Family Reunion*, J. M. Dent & Sons Ltd., and Curtis Brown Ltd., New York.

John Betjeman: 'Harvest Hymn' from *High and Low*, and 'Hunter Trials' from *Collected Poems*, John Murray Ltd.

S. V. Benet: 'Portrait of a Boy', the Estate of the late S. V. Benet. © 1917 by Stephen Vincent Benet. © renewed 1945 by Rosemary Carr Benet.

A. E. Housman: 'Eight o'Clock' from *Collected Poems*, the Society of Authors as the literary representative of the Estate of A. E. Housman, and Messrs. Jonathan Cape Ltd.

Tony Connor: 'Child's Bouncing Song'.

Vachel Lindsay: 'The Daniel Jazz', 'The Sea Serpent Chantey' and 'The Congo' from *Collected Poems*, Macmillan.

Andrew Young: 'Hard Frost', 'Snow' and 'The Beech', from *Collected Poems*, Rupert Hart-Davis.

John Heath-Stubbs: 'The Gecko', 'The Hare' and 'The Tortoise' from *Collected Poems*, Oxford University Press.

Phoebe Hesketh: 'The Heron' from *Prayer for the Sun*, Oxford University Press.

Every effort has been made to trace the copyright owners of Arnold Bennett's *Young Man of Montrose*.

The Authors wish to thank the following for permission to reproduce photographs:

R. A. Haynes: 'Eye of a bee', 'Peacock', 'Dandelion head', 'Bees' and 'Human eye'.

Wadsworth Atheneum, Hartford: 'Apparition of a face and a fruit-dish on a beach', Salvador Dali.

Salford Corporation and Neville Cooper: 'Market scene, Northern town', Lowry.

Neville Cooper: 'Bath-time'.

A. D. S. Macpherson: 'Bus queue in Stirling'.

The Mansell Collection: Da Vinci's 'Medusa', Alinari; 'Dancer with a bouquet', Degas.

National Gallery of Art, Washington D.C., Rosenwald Collection: 'The cry', Edward Munch.

J. Allen Cash: 'Snow on a twig'.

The Times Newspaper: 'Fog'.

The Associated Press: 'Up to space'.

Scottish Daily Mail: 'Old and new bridges – Firth of Forth'.

The Guardian: 'Boys fishing'.

Canadian Government Travel Bureau: 'Niagara Falls'.

Kunsthistorisches Museum: 'Der Sommer', Arcimboldo.

We wish to thank our mother and our wives for the very considerable help they have given in the preparation of the typescript.

M. G. B.
P. B.

ISBN 0 340 06964 3

First printed 1969
Reprinted 1970
Second edition 1972

Copyright © 1969, 1972 M. G. Benton and P. Benton
All rights reserved. No part of this
publication may be reproduced or transmitted in
any form or by any means, electronic or
mechanical, including photocopy, recording, or
any information storage and retrieval system,
without permission in writing from the publisher.

The English Universities Press Ltd
St Paul's House, Warwick Lane, London EC4P 4AH

Printed in Great Britain by
Butler & Tanner Ltd, Frome and London

198